PENTECOSTAL PIONEER:

*The Life and Legacy of
Rudy Esperanza in the Early Years
of the Assemblies of God
in the Philippines*

Dynnice Rosanny D. Engcoy

WIPF & STOCK · Eugene, Oregon

Wipf and Stock Publishers
199 W 8th Ave, Suite 3
Eugene, OR 97401

Pentecostal Pioneer
The Life and Legacy of Rudy Esperanza in the Early Years
of the Assemblies of God in the Philippines
By Engcoy, Dynnice Rosanny D.
Copyright©2014 APTS Press and Dynnice Rosanny D. Engcoy
ISBN 13: 978-1-5326-1420-0
Publication date 10/27/2017
Previously published by APTS Press, 2014

This edition is published by Wipf and Stock Publishers
under license from APTS Press.

Publisher's Preface

With this new volume we are pleased to restart our Pentecostalism Around the World series, of which this book is volume 4. The purpose of this series is to provide a place for historical reflection on what God is doing through the Pentecostal Movement, particularly in the Asia Pacific and Pacific Oceana regions of the world.

The three previous titles are, *Reflections of an Early American Pentecostal* by Stanley Horton, *The Cross Among Pagodas: A History of the Assemblies of God in Myanmar* by Chin Khua Khai, and *Pentecost to the Uttermost: A History of the Assemblies of God in Samoa* by Tavita Pagaialii. These books are available at the APTS Bookstore on our Baguio Campus and at the ICI Bookstore in Valenzuela City in Metro Manila.

In publishing this book, Dr. Rose Engcoy becomes the first Filipino to publish a book with APTS Press and we offer her our heartiest congratulations.

THE PUBLISHER

Author's Preface

Sometimes negative emotions can lead to positive actions. While working at the Asia Pacific Research Center archives in Baguio, I found out that the Philippines General Council of the Assemblies of God (PGCAG) did not yet have a book on its history. Some other much younger AG General Councils in Asia had their book, but not us. Honestly, I felt sad and jealous.

We do have records of the PGCAG's early history, but they are mostly reports and letters sent back to the United States by American AG missionaries assigned to the Philippines. As expected, the reports are on the American missionaries' activities and contributions. Many times, the participation of local Filipino workers are only mentioned in passing. One of the early Filipino ministers did write a masters thesis on the subject back in 1965, but it was never published.

My sadness and jealousy turned into a desire to write the PGCAG history. I wanted people to know what God had done in and through the lives of "imperfect saints" so that the PGCAG became one of the fastest growing denominations in the Philippines at the beginning of the 21st century.[1] Moreover, I wanted to present historical data from a Filipino pioneer's viewpoint.

To learn how to write the PGCAG history properly, I took advanced studies in Church History with the Asia Graduate School of Theology (AGST). At AGST, I realized that writing the history of the PGCAG was too broad for me to handle. Thus, I narrowed my research on one Filipino AG pioneer, Rev. Rodrigo Cabanilla Esperanza. As the first Filipino to hold the highest position in the Assemblies of God, and the one to stay longest to date in that top position, Esperanza played an important role in forming the young denomination.

This book is based on my AGST dissertation. With the history of the PGCAG as the background, I explore major roles that Esperanza played from 1940, which marked the birth of Assemblies of God work in the Philippines, to 1969, the year he died. I limit myself to discussing events in his life which impacted the PGCAG's pioneering years, especially his contributions that continue to influence the PGCAG in the twenty-first century. Many of my sources were conversations with people who knew Esperanza or were directly influenced by him. Please note that there are cases when dates, places, and events may not be perfectly accurate. People tend to forget some of those details. However, interviews are the best way to know what the past meant to people and how it felt to be a part of those times.[2]

Through this book, I aim to promote a greater understanding of and appreciation for the role of local pioneers in building the Filipino Pentecostal church. Sadly, many Filipinos have no idea who the Pentecostal pioneers in the Philippines were, much less what they went through to ensure that we would have the Pentecostal gospel in our generation. No wonder many contemporary Filipinos do not appreciate their Pentecostal legacy.

Moreover, I hope to encourage present-day Filipinos, especially AG constituents, to engage in further historical research to better understand their roots which helped form the character of their denomination. May this book be a catalyst for more historical research and writing on Filipino Pentecostal legacy.

Lastly, I hope this book would be a source of historical insights for present-day PGCAG leaders. May these insights help them to better understand the PGCAG's formative years and to come up with more effective strategies for the further growth of the Assemblies of God in the Philippines.

Should this book cause faith to arise in the hearts of the present generation of Filipino Pentecostals to do greater exploits in these last days, then it would be worth all the effort and sacrifice in writing it.

To God be all the glory!

Rose Engcoy
October 2014

---

[1]John W. Kennedy, "The Philippines: Embracing the Challenge," *Pentecostal Evangel*, 4 June 2000, 5. "Largest Denominations: Philippines," *DAWN Philippines: A Report on the State of the Evangelical Churches in the Philippines 2000*, with a foreword by Bishop Efraim M. Tendero (n.p. and n.d.), 40.

[2]Texas Historical Commission, "Fundamentals of Oral History: Texas Preservation Guidelines," available at http://www.thc.state.tx.us/publications/guidelines/OralHistory.pdf, accessed January 10, 2012.

Foreword

Rose Engcoy's insightful study of the life and ministry of Rodrigo ("Rudy") Esperanza is important for two reasons.

The first is that all of us have much to learn from Rev. Esperanza's example. After all, he was one of the pioneers of Pentecostalism in the Philippines. His work as a church planter, pastor, educator, and long-time senior administrator of the Philippines General Council of the Assemblies of God (PGCAG) was vitally important to that denomination's early success which has situated it in the front ranks of the community of Spirit-filled believers in his beloved homeland.

Rev. Esperanza played a role in the PGCAG rather like that played by J. Roswell Flower during the Assemblies' formative years in the United States. Both men were irenic bridge-builders. Rev. Flower, who took the lead in keeping the Assemblies committed to Trinitarian orthodoxy, went on to foster fraternal relations with other Pentecostal denominations and even with non-Pentecostal evangelicals, playing a pivotal role in the founding of the National Association of Evangelicals.[1]

Similarly, Rev. Esperanza, a veteran ecclesiastical firefighter who doused the flames of many a conflict that threatened to disrupt the PGCAG's unity, not only helped to pilot the United Pentecostal Fellowship but also led his fellow Pentecostals in collaboration with non-Pentecostal evangelicals in a range of evangelistic and ministry activities that went a long way toward allaying suspicions on both sides. Growing churches are always the most vulnerable to conflict and schism, so Christians who long for unity in the body of Christ can learn a lot from Rev. Esperanza. This book will help with that.

But Dr. Engcoy's study is important for another reason as well. Today the Christian community is growing rapidly in Asia, especially East Asia, rivaling the explosive growth of the church in Africa.[2]

Riding the crest of the wave are Pentecostal denominations like the PGCAG. In fact, missiologist David Barrett estimates that 80 percent of East Asia's Christians are Pentecostal or Charismatic.[3] Something similar is happening here in the Philippines, with the evangelical community growing steadily since the 1970s and today making up roughly 10 percent of the nation's population.[4] Most Philippine evangelicals are Pentecostal or Charismatic, and, thanks to the impact of organizations like Mike Velarde's El Shaddai, in the Philippines even the Catholic Church is taking on an increasingly Charismatic cast.

Just as Katharine Wiegele's study of Brother Mike and El Shaddai gives us a good idea of what lies ahead for Philippine Catholicism,[5] Rose Engcoy's study of Rudy Esperanza and the early years of the PGCAG gives us a good idea of what lies ahead for Philippine Protestantism. Together they give us an excellent idea of what lies ahead for Asian Christianity. I find that enormously encouraging.

George W. Harper, Ph.D.
Asia Graduate School of Theology
Quezon City, Philippines

---

[1]Gary B. McGee, "Flower, Joseph James Roswell (1888-1970) and Alice Reynolds (1890-1991)," in *New International Dictionary of Pentecostal and Charismatic Movements*, rev. ed.

[2]Peter Brierley, *Future Church: A Global Analysis of the Christian Community to the Year 2010* (Oxford, England: Monarch, 1998), 20-21.

[3]David B. Barrett, "Annual Statistical Table on Global Mission: 1989," *International Bulletin of Missionary Research* 13, no. 1 (January 1989): 20.

[4]George W. Harper, "Philippine Tongues of Fire? Latin American Pentecostalism and the Future of Filipino Christianity," *Evangelical Review of Theology* 26, no. 2 (April 2002): 153-180.

[5]Katharine L. Wiegele, *Investing in Miracles: El Shaddai and the Transformation of Popular Catholicism in the Philippines* (Honolulu: University of Hawai'i Press, 2005).

Acknowledgments

The seed of this research was planted in my heart in 2000 when I accepted Dr. Paul Lewis's invitation to serve at the Asia Pacific Research Center (APRC) at the Asia Pacific Theological Seminary (APTS) in Baguio City, Philippines. As I worked on the PGCAG holdings in the archives, the desire to educate the Filipino AG constituents about what our pioneers had done to ensure that the Pentecostal message would be passed on to succeeding generations gave me impetus to embark on further studies in church history. As I researched, certain persons and organizations gave me "wind beneath my wings" to press on until I finished my dissertation. I would like to acknowledge the following:

Dr. Paul Lewis, former APRC director, who believed in my vision and supported me all the way; Dr. Wonsuk Ma and Dr. Julie Ma, who gave me their constant support and encouragement; my AGTS advisers—Dr. Rodrigo Tano, Dr. Timothy Gener, and Dr. George Harper—who made sure that my program was completed; my AGST professors—Dr. Floyd Cunningham, Dr. Adonis Gorospe, Dr. Azriel Azarcon, and Dr. Anne Kwantes—who gave me invaluable guidance in synthesizing my dissertation; Dr. George Harper, who saw to the accuracy of what I wrote and whose "eagle eyes" saw typos that my computer failed to detect; and my dissertation editors, Laura DeCorte and Dr. Steve Langston. This book is an abridged edition of that dissertation.

Heartfelt thanks to Noel and Anna Manayon, who took and edited all the videos of the Rodolfo Esperanza Documentary Project; Lydia Esperanza Javier and Rebecca Lagmay Alimbuyao, who provided family photos and arranged for the interviews with Rev. Esperanza's relatives; Dr. Joseph Suico, who, in his capacity as PGCAG General Secretary, granted me access to the PGCAG archives; the PGCAG executives and Rev. William Snider, who gave financial support for the Rodolfo Esperanza Documentary Project; and Roberto and Kathleen Garciano, my brother-in-law and sister, who never failed to welcome me into their home during the many years of my studies in Manila.

I want to thank the APTS AdCom, who approved the sponsorship of my graduate studies under the seminary's faculty development program, and Dr. Theresa Lua, AGST Dean, who provided scholarship assistance so that I could finish my dissertation.

This book could not have been published were it not for the perseverance of the APTS Press Director, Dr. Dave Johnson, and the diligent editing and formatting of the book's Project Director, Lindsay Crabtree. Thank you also to APRC's resident archivist, William Alcabedos, for his patient help in looking up documents and photos.

Finally, thank you to my family, friends, and churches, who were my faithful prayer partners all these years.

To all of you, I express my deep gratitude. May God multiply back to you what you have so generously shared with me as I journeyed through this research and writing.

Dedication

This book is dedicated to three special groups of people:

- my family: Lem, GJ, and Hazel, who unconditionally supported me with their love, encouragement, and prayers, and gave me time and space as I focused on finishing this work, especially in the last few months;

- my mentors: Dr. and Mrs. Gary and Doris Denbow, who were my spiritual parents from the beginning of my ministry, and Dr. and Mrs. Eleazer and Esther Javier, who guided and supported me in my calling to preserve the PGCAG legacy;

   and

- all the PGCAG pioneers who, together with Reverend Rodrigo Esperanza, blazed the trail. May their sacrifices also be told by the succeeding generations. Most of all, may we who come after them learn from their wisdom, gained from their selfless commitment to the ministry, so we may better serve our Master and likewise hear the word, *"Well done, good and faithful servant."*

Contents

Chapter 1	Introduction	1
Chapter 2	Background and Birth of the Assemblies of God USA	9
Chapter 3	Background and Birth of the PGCAG	25
Chapter 4	Esperanza's Background	53
Chapter 5	Foundational Roles in the PGCAG	63
Chapter 6	District Secretary and General Superintendent	75
Chapter 7	Personal Leadership Qualities	93
Chapter 8	Visionary Leader	115
Chapter 9	Assessment of Esperanza's Leadership Role and Influence	143
Chapter 10	Conclusions and Recommendations	161
Endnotes		173
Bibliography		191

Chapter 1

Rev. Rodrigo "Rudy" C. Esperanza
District Secretary, 1940-1946
District Superintendent, 1946-1953
General Superintendent, 1953-1969
Source: PGCAG Headquarters, BBC Compound, Malinta, Valenzuela City

INTRODUCTION

Rodrigo Esperanza's impact on the Assemblies of God in the Philippines cannot be overstated. In his various roles as pastor, denominational leader, evangelist, writer, radio host, and Bible school teacher, Esperanza built the foundation for the modern-day Philippines General Council of the Assemblies of God (PGCAG). Much of the movement's growth can be traced back to the work of this great pioneer. This book is dedicated to examining the life and work of Esperanza and his impact on the Assemblies of God in the Philippines. However, before we can delve into the life and background of Esperanza, we must focus on the history of the Assemblies of God both in the United States and also in the Philippines. Only with the movement's background firmly in focus can we truly appreciate Esperanza's ongoing legacy.

From the time Crispulo Garsulao, the first Filipino Assemblies of God pioneer, arrived back on Philippine soil in 1928 to the turn of the twenty-first century, the Assemblies of God in the Philippines has grown by leaps and bounds.[1] Historian Arthur Tuggy gives the following statistics:

> By 1949, 1822 members were reported. In 1952 there were 2,193. Then the Assemblies of God entered a new phase of rapid growth as the large Bethel Temple in Manila was begun under the ministry of Lester Sumrall. This church, which became the largest Protestant church in Manila, had its beginning...in 1952 and 1953....By 1958, the Assemblies of God reported a membership of 12,022—an increase of almost 500 percent in five years![2]

Wonsuk Ma reports further:

> Efforts were made to expand the ministry through evangelism and church-planting programs, especially in cities and towns. By 1979 there were 1,195 ministers, 383 churches, 16 training schools, and two cross-cultural missionaries. The next 10 years, however, proved to be a turning point for the denomination. By the end of the 1980s the number of churches had more than tripled: 1,329 churches with 2,022 ministers, 20 training schools, and 4 overseas missionaries. This was a time of social and political unrest, and also a period of explosive growth, particularly among the [P]entecostal and [C]harismatic segments of Philippine Christianity.[3]

John Kennedy declares that at the turn of this century the PGCAG has "2,600 churches attended by 430,830 people, making it the largest evangelical body" in the predominantly Roman

Catholic Asian country.[4] In September 2001, Discipling a Whole Nation (DAWN) Philippines issued statistics placing the PGCAG with its 2,853 churches at the top of its ranking of Philippine Protestant denominations by number of congregations.[5]

In its three-quarters of a century of existence in this country, the PGCAG has experienced many ups and downs. First of all, when the Americans took over the Philippines, its population was, as it still is, primarily Roman Catholic. Furthermore, before the coming of Mr. and Mrs. Benjamin Caudle, Assemblies of God missionaries who brought the Pentecostal message in 1926,[6] other Protestant denominations had already established their bulwarks in the Philippines by means of the Comity arrangement of April 1901. In the arrangement, representatives of seven missionary and Bible societies formed the Evangelical Union of the Philippine Islands, which assigned specific geographical areas to each member of the Union.[7] As the AG came much later, it was not part of this agreement. To make matters worse, in the early decades of the twentieth century, Pentecostals were still generally disfavored in the United States. Noted American evangelist R. A. Torrey issued this pronouncement: "The Movement as a whole has apparently developed more immorality than any other modern movement except spiritism, to which it is so closely allied in many ways."[8] This negative attitude in the US was carried over to the Philippines. The Pentecostal newcomers were not welcomed. They were socially ostracized and persecuted not only by the Roman Catholics but also by the evangelical community. Many AG pioneers were mocked during street meetings or threatened with court cases or physical harm. A few were actually attacked. Many also endured the stoning of their churches while they were holding worship services. Even evangelicals would not allow members of their families to attend Pentecostal services.[9] Filipino AG pioneers urgently requested a representative from the United States AG to come and organize the group in the Philippines to give them a legal identity.

Despite persecution, the group's membership continued to multiply. However, three major conflicts—the split of the Manila Bethel Temple in 1965, the split of the denomination in 1973, and a further split in 1980[10]—hampered the phenomenal growth of the Assemblies of God. James H. Montgomery reports that the denomination lost its momentum during these conflicts, yet the group continued to grow, although not as fast as before.[11] Moreover, as Ma reports in the above quotation, by the end of the 1980s, the PGCAG had more than tripled the number of its churches, doubled the number of its ministers, and increased the number of its training schools and overseas missionaries.

Statement of the Problem

Why did the PGCAG experience phenomenal growth in spite of seasons of major conflict within the organization? What role did the PGCAG's leaders play in steering the denomination along a path for growth? What leadership style exerted a major influence in the group's pioneering years? My hypothesis is that Rodrigo Esperanza's many pioneering roles—pastor, denominational leader, evangelist, writer, radio host, Bible school teacher, etc., were foundational to the Assemblies of God in the Philippines and set the leadership pattern which helped propel the fledgling denomination into rapid numerical growth.

Statement of Purpose

In my reading of the history of various Protestant groups in the Philippines for a course on Philippine Protestantism, three main factors stood out as keys to their growth.[12] The first two factors were the presence of Bible schools and the availability of denominational literature and other publications. However, the third factor, the presence of good denominational leaders, was the most significant. These leaders served as catalysts for their groups' growth. Their lives and ministries became role models for their contemporaries and succeeding generations. They were goal-setters, pioneers, and innovators, leading their groups to attempt bigger tasks and achieve higher goals. Without the support of good denominational leaders, Bible schools and denominational literature could not exist. Among the PGCAG pioneers, none played a greater role than Reverend Rodrigo "Rudy" Esperanza, the first PGCAG General Superintendent.

This book aims to explore the various roles that Esperanza played from 1940, which marked the birth of the Assemblies of God work in the Philippines, to 1969, the year he died. It further aims to demonstrate Esperanza's influence during the PGCAG's pioneering years and trace the ways in which his leadership continues to impact the denomination in the twenty-first century.

Significance of the Study

The majority of the records of the PGCAG's early history are reports and correspondence sent back to the United States by General Council of the Assemblies of God (henceforth, USAG) missionaries assigned to the Philippines. As such, these records reflect the American missionaries' viewpoints and primarily focus on their contributions. Many times, the participation and contributions of local workers are only mentioned in passing; at times they are not mentioned at all.

Various PGCAG district leaders have sought to make up for this lack by writing the history of their own districts. These district histories appropriately stress the contributions of Filipino pioneers. However, the said histories have often been written without attention to scholarly historical methodologies, thus casting doubt on the credibility of their accounts.

This book will present the life of Reverend Rodrigo Esperanza with the history of the PGCAG as the backdrop. As such, it will be written from a Filipino pioneer's viewpoint. Through this book, I aim to promote a greater understanding and appreciation of the role of local pioneers in building the PGCAG. Moreover, I desire to encourage present-day Filipinos, especially AG constituents, to engage in further historical research to better understand their roots which helped form the ethos and character of their denomination. Most of all, I hope this book will be a source of historical insights for present-day PGCAG leaders to help them not only to better understand the PGCAG's formative years but also to formulate better plans and more effective strategies for the further growth of the Assemblies of God in the Philippines.

Delimitation

As previously stated, this book will be limited to the roles of Rodrigo Esperanza in the PGCAG from 1940 to 1969. Therefore, only those events or issues in the history of the denomination in which Esperanza had directly participated or exerted influence on will be included in this book. A more exhaustive research on the PGCAG's history will have to be dealt with in another book. The limitations of oral history research, one of the methods used in gathering information for this paper, also need to be kept in mind.

To ascertain the roles of Esperanza that were foundational to the Assemblies of God in the Philippines and the lasting impact of those roles, this book will focus on the following questions:

- What was Esperanza's formative background?
- What roles did he play in the history of the PGCAG?
- What factors influenced him in fulfilling his roles?
- What lasting impact did he have on the PGCAG?
- What benefits can the present PGCAG leaders receive from studying his leadership roles?

Methodology

For this study, I have conducted historical research to ascertain the influence of Rudy Esperanza that sculpted the leadership model of the early PGCAG. The historical research involved both literature and field research.

Literature Research

In my capacity as archivist of the Asia Pacific Research Center (APRC) since 2000, I have access to primary and secondary sources dealing with the history of Pentecostal denominations in the Philippines, especially the PGCAG. Other vital sources of information are the records kept in the PGCAG national headquarters archives in Metro Manila and in the USAG archives, most especially the Flower Pentecostal Heritage Center and the Assemblies of God World Missions archives, both at the USAG headquarters in Springfield, Missouri. Also available are early PGCAG publications and PGCAG Bible schools' and districts' publications. The library and archives of De La Salle University Taft, Ateneo the Manila University, and University of San Carlos in Cebu were important sources of information on the sociological, economic, and political conditions prevailing in the Philippines during the timeframe covered in this book.

Oral History

I also used as sources the holdings of the APRC Oral History archives, an ongoing project of the APRC. Although the majority of Filipinos are literate, "the country has maintained its oral cognitive orientation, as witnessed by the lack of a sizable reading population and a brilliant oral culture in universities which rarely gets transcribed into written form."[13] I conducted the majority of the nearly fifty interviews already transcribed employing standard methods for oral history interviews to gather data from Pentecostal church pioneers, their family and friends, and local observers.

The field research also yielded a considerable quantity of photos, printed matter, and other documents kept by the pioneer or his/her family in private family archives. Said archival materials were rich sources of information on the early days of the denomination in the Philippines. Other local churches and districts gladly donated to the APRC write-ups of their respective histories.

As this research demonstrates, the footprints of the PGCAG's pioneers are clearly seen through the movement's history, none more than Reverend Rodrigo "Rudy" Esperanza. To fully appreciate Esperanza's past and continuing influence in the Assemblies of God in the Philippines, let us turn our attention to the birth of its parent organization, the Assemblies of God in America.

Chapter 2

First General Council of the Assemblies of God, Hot Springs, Arkansas, April 2-12, 1914
Source: Google Images, accessed September 30, 2014

BACKGROUND AND BIRTH
OF THE ASSEMBLIES OF GOD USA

In *Historical and Theological Background*, Allan Anderson traces the characteristic features of Pentecostalism from the first-century church up to the present. He notices an increase of charismata among radical Protestants in the nineteenth century, especially among the Methodist and Holiness movements. He points out that although there were earlier revivals in Europe and North America that prepared the soil for the Pentecostal revival, there were also revivals with charismatic features in Asia, Africa, and Latin America that were not directly related to the revivals in North America. All of these early-twentieth-century revivals, however, had common features: "intense desire to pray, emotional confession of sins, manifestations of the coming of the Spirit, successful and accelerated evangelism, and spiritual gifts to confirm that the power of the Spirit had come. Bolstered by earlier revival movements in the nineteenth century... this coming of the Spirit was linked to a belief that the last days had come, and that the gospel was to be preached to all the nations of earth before the soon coming of the Lord."[1]

Like many other historians, William Kay looks to the nineteenth century to trace the history of Pentecostalism. Moreover, like Anderson, he traces the beginnings of Pentecostalism in other countries independent of North America. He includes Pentecostalism in Latin America, Europe, Africa, and Asia, and underscores the Pentecostal interconnections between these continents.[2] However, as I will demonstrate later, Rudy Esperanza's story and the beginnings of the Assemblies of God in the Philippines are deeply rooted in the Pentecostal Movement in America, and particularly in the Assemblies of God fellowship that came into being there. Thus, we shall leave the history of the Pentecostal movement in these places to other scholars.

Birth of Modern Pentecostalism in the United States

Many historians point to two major revivals as the origin of modern Pentecostalism in America. The first was the revival in Topeka, Kansas, led by Charles Parham at the turn of the twentieth century. The second was the revival at Azusa Street, Los Angeles, led by William Seymour beginning in 1906. Much has been written about both of these revivals so I will only briefly sketch them here.

Parham was a white American evangelist and theologian who held the conviction that the apostolic faith was being restored to the church. He opened Bethel Bible School in Topeka, Kansas, in October 1900 to teach and further explore this belief.[3] Parham believed that the experience of Spirit baptism was the assurance that one would join the rapture and escape the tribulation.[4] Moreover, it was "eschatologically necessary for world evangelization."[5] Due to these beliefs, he became interested in studying the baptism of the Holy Spirit and identifying the biblical evidence that one had received the experience.[6]

Parham instructed his students to search the Scriptures in Acts 2 to ascertain whether there was any biblical evidence that one had indeed received the baptism of the Holy Spirit.[7] His students discovered that the biblical evidence for the baptism of the Holy Spirit was speaking in tongues. In the early morning hours of January 1, 1901, one of the students, Agnes Ozman, asked that Parham lay his hands on her so she would receive the baptism, just as the Scriptures stated. In a few moments, she started to speak in tongues. The others were encouraged and sought the same experience. Soon many of the students received the baptism with speaking in tongues. Three days later, Parham himself also spoke in tongues.[8]

After receiving the baptism of the Holy Spirit and speaking in tongues, Charles Parham embarked on a series of crusades preaching what he came to believe as the true "apostolic faith." Edith Blumhofer notes that Parham's teaching that tongues would facilitate world evangelization led him to emphasize missions.[9] In December 1905, he founded a school, in Houston, Texas, to train missionary evangelists. It was this school that an African American Holiness preacher, William Joseph Seymour, came to attend.[10]

In an African American church in Houston, Seymour heard Lucy Farrow, the cook for Parham's Bible school,[11] speak in tongues. He asked Farrow about her gift and she introduced him to Parham. Seymour, who was an African American, asked permission to join the school. Parham, who did not like black people, initially hesitated, but later agreed to admit Seymour. Despite discrimination, Seymour received Parham's teachings on the baptism of the Holy Spirit with the evidence of speaking in tongues. Soon Seymour was preaching the same all over Houston although he himself had not yet received the experience.[12]

On February 22, 1906, Seymour arrived in Los Angeles at the invitation of Julia W. Hutchins, a woman who had formed her own Holiness church after being ushered out of her Baptist congregation because she was preaching a baptism of the Holy Spirit subsequent to conversion.[13] On his first Sunday, Seymour spoke on the baptism of the Holy Spirit with the accompanying evidence of speaking in tongues, just as he had learned from Parham. Hutchins was so disturbed by this teaching that when Seymour returned to preach in the afternoon, he found that she had padlocked the church.[14]

Unperturbed, Seymour stayed with Edward Lee, one of Hutchins' members, and conducted Bible studies with a small group of followers in the house of Arthur and Ruth Asberry, at 214 North Bonnie Brae Street.[15] Soon, African Americans and white Americans were attending the meetings, "and high on their agenda was prayer for revival and an expectation that God was about to move in their midst."[16]

The much-longed-for day finally arrived. Cecil Robeck recounts the event as follows:

> On Monday, Apr. 9, 1906, before Seymour left Edward Lee to go to the Asberry home for the evening meeting, Lee told him of a vision that he had had in which the apostles showed him how to speak in tongues. The two men prayed together, and in moments Lee was speaking in tongues. Seymour carried the news to his meeting on Bonnie Brae, where Jennie Evans Moore and several others also broke into tongues. News spread rapidly, and people came to Bonnie Brae to see and hear for themselves. Within a week the group had rented 312 Azusa Street, and the mission had begun.[17]

Robeck details the rapid expansion of the Azusa revival. Just a few days after its opening, the Azusa Street mission house was packed and overflowing with people. Baptismal services at the beach regularly had from 150 to 250 baptismal candidates. Evangelistic zeal generated by the mission was such that members and sympathizers planted similar congregations in surrounding communities and even sent evangelists to preach along the West Coast. By December of the same year, they already had evangelists in New York City. That same month, missionary zeal led at least thirteen missionaries to Africa. A month later, in January 1907, the mission's missionaries were in Mexico, Canada, Western Europe, the Middle East, West Africa, and several countries in Asia. By 1908, missionaries had reached South Africa, Central and Eastern Europe, and as far as northern Russia.[18]

In view of the Azusa revival's outcome, some church historians declare that the growth of the Pentecostal movement is unprecedented, exceeding that of "old-line Protestant denominations." They believe that "the Pentecostal revival ranks in importance with the establishment of the Apostolic Church and with the Protestant Reformation."[19] With the widespread international influence of the Azusa Street mission, it is no wonder many historians consider it as the birthplace of Pentecostalism. However, for those who consider chronology and theology as more important, they point to Topeka, Kansas as the place which gave birth to modern Pentecostalism. But not all was well with the fast-growing movement.

Birth of the United States Assemblies of God

At the turn of the twentieth century, the majority of Pentecostals, especially those coming from the Azusa revival, were rejected by their own traditional denominations. Missionaries who embraced Pentecostalism were dismissed by their mission boards. The pain of this rejection created in these Pentecostals an aversion to any organizational structure imposed upon their new-found faith.[20] They claimed, "We have been delivered from denominationalism."[21] In fact, according to Walter J. Hollenweger, "For the earliest Pentecostals it was more important to pray than to organize...The first Pentecostals rejected every kind of organization."[22]

However, Klaude Kendrick notes that some minimal organization was needed to avoid total anarchy and confusion that could cause the disintegration of the movement, because "each person regarded himself as the final authority between heaven and earth," pointing to ever more profound knowledge and ever more glorious experiences of salvation as the basis for that authority.[23]

Moreover, as the new movement grew, other issues and problems surfaced that increasingly needed a united response and cooperation among the various Pentecostal congregations and ministries. Some contemplated the idea of forming a loose organization or fellowship, but

> [t]hey did not intend to create a denomination, nor did they expect longevity for themselves or their movement. They hoped only to conserve what they understood to be the core of the Pentecostal message and to preserve the movement's sense of history and identity during a brief burst of evangelism that would culminate in Christ's soon return.[24]

Reasons for Organizing

William Menzies succinctly deals with the reasons why some Pentecostal leaders saw the need to organize the movement:[25]

1. *Expulsion from the churches.* Pentecostals were rejected not only by the Holiness Movement and Fundamentalism but also by the rest of Christianity. The following reasons were given for the rejection: too much display of emotions; lack of social respectability, since there were almost no notable or influential personalities among them; negative press reports, which created fear of Pentecostals in people's hearts; divisive attitude of Pentecostals, who looked down on non-Pentecostals' spirituality, thus causing ill feelings.

2. *Practical needs.* The Church of God in Christ, under Bishop Mason, was legally incorporated and was eligible for reduced clergy fares on the Southern railroads. Thus, some ministers joined this Pentecostal group between 1910 to 1914, "mainly for purposes of business."[26]

3. *Partisanship.* Clusters of young ministers gathered around strong Pentecostal leaders, producing a divisive and partisan spirit.

4. *Local abuses.* Local churches were sometimes "fleeced" by men posing as Pentecostal preachers. Since ordination was virtually unknown, no one bothered to check credentials.

5. *Missionary cooperation.* Mission zeal saw many missionaries go to foreign lands, some without credentials, supervision, or financial accountability. Also, missionaries abroad lacked proper financing, legal

representation, correlation of work, and endorsement for holding property.

6. *Doctrinal problems.* Many untrained ministers were hard-pressed to feed an established flock for very long, so some simply moved on to new congregations. Others sought to make up for their lack by getting "new revelations," whose contents often produced confusion and disarray. Moreover, the constant stream of periodicals emanating from diverse locations, sometimes with conflicting emphases, and the lack of uniformity in methodology and practice heightened the feeling of growing chaos as 1914 approached.

Although recognizing the great opposition to their plans to organize, a group of Pentecostal leaders called for a "General Convention of Pentecostal Saints and Churches of God in Christ" in the old Grand Opera House at Hot Springs, Arkansas, from April 2 to 12, 1914. The call was "to all the churches of God in Christ, to all Pentecostal or Apostolic Faith Assemblies who desire with united purpose to co-operate in love and peace to push the interests of the kingdom of God everywhere."[27]

Purpose of Organization

The following are excerpts of the purposes for the convention lifted from the announcement above:[28]

First – set a better understanding of what God would have us teach, that we may do away with so many divisions, both in doctrines and in the various names under which our Pentecostal people are working and incorporating.

Second – that we know how to conserve the work, that we may all build up and not tear down, both in home and foreign lands.

Third – that we may get a better understanding of the needs of each foreign field, and may know how to place our money in such a way that one mission or missionary shall not suffer, while another not any more worthy, lives in luxuries [sic]. Also that we may discourage wasting money on those who are running here and there accomplishing nothing, and may concentrate our support on those who mean business for our King.

Fourth – Many of the saints have felt the need of chartering the churches of God in Christ, putting them on a legal basis, and thus *obeying the laws of* the land," as God says...[B]ecause of this many assemblies have already chartered under different names as a *local* work, in both home and foreign lands. Why not charter under *one Bible name*, 2 Thes. 2-14. [sic] Thus [sic] eliminating another phase of division in Pentecostal work?

Fifth – We may also have a proposition to lay before the body for a general Bible Training School with a literary department for our people.

First General Council – Hot Springs, Arkansas, 1914

As expected, the announcement stirred up a controversy. Despite the theological unity reflected in the fact that "[t]he first council had been convened by people who had concluded by 1910 that, in doctrinal terms, holiness was not a 'second blessing' but a process of growth and change,"[29] those who attended the convention were polarized on another issue. Some saw the need for united effort while others feared compromise and the possibility that people might return to denominationalism.

Nevertheless, both camps showed up at the convention. Of the more than 300 attendees coming from twenty states, 128 were ministers and missionaries.[30] Wisely, the convenors spent the first three days in spiritual feeding and worship, dispelling fears that organization would prematurely end the move of the Holy Spirit in their midst. Only on the fourth day did the business meetings begin. Kendrick believes that this early "conditioning" could have helped pave the way for the people to achieve the goals of the convention.[31]

At the convention, several resolutions were submitted and passed and a "Preamble and Resolution on Constitution" was accepted. The *Word and Witness*, adopted as the official organ of the Assemblies of God, reported on that historical agreement:

> This was a most remarkable manifestation of the presence and guidance of the Spirit of God in the camp. Neither [of the camps] knew what the other would do, but each was determined not to organize a man-made church and charter it as a new sect in the land. Great indeed was the presence of God to bring out as one in purpose, principles and unity what men supposed to be two diverse crowds.[32]

The Constitutional Declaration of the newly formed fellowship unanimously accepted the name "General Council of the Assemblies of God."[33] The Preamble to Constitution was approved by the convention, though the drawing up and adoption of a constitution would come more than a decade later.

Controversies

Although the newly formed council (they refused to be called a "denomination") parted company in apparent agreement and unity, one inherent characteristic of Pentecostals during the time left the door wide open for future conflicts. Pentecostals saw the receiving of "new revelations" as a sign of spirituality. In fact, E. N. Bell, member of the elected Executive Presbytery and editor of *Word and Witness*,[34] declared, "We must keep our skylights open so as not to reject any new light God may throw upon the old Word. We must not fail to keep pace in life or teaching with light from heaven."[35] A pastor who did not receive such revelations was seen as not being in touch with the Spirit of God, leaving his or her spirituality in question. Since such divine revelations were connected to divine approval, Pentecostals vigorously defended them. It was such a belief that opened the door for internal conflicts in the new group. Three controversies that had started before the birth of the organization soon came to a climax. Despite the group's refusal to come up with creeds or doctrines, all three issues dealt with doctrines.[36]

The "Second Blessing"

Since the first General Council of the Assemblies of God in Hot Springs, Arkansas chose not to formulate a statement of faith, members had liberty to adhere to varied doctrines. Most of the members believed in progressive sanctification, yet many still held to the second-blessing theology of sanctification. This resulted in internal dissension. "Holiness Pentecostals charged Pentecostals who rejected crisis sanctification with heresy."[37] In an effort to quell the controversy, the Assemblies of God issued an official statement in 1916 that was couched in words acceptable to both camps. However, over the course of time, the denomination slowly moved away from the Holiness theology of sanctification.[38]

The Oneness Controversy

A greater controversy that threatened the two-year-old denomination with "almost complete disaster" arose over the proper formula to be used during water baptism.[39] This controversy escalated into a debate over the nature of the Godhead.

In April 1913, at a Pentecostal camp meeting in Arroyo Seco, near Los Angeles, one of the speakers, R. E. McAlister, shared an observation that "the apostles invariably baptized their converts once in the name of Jesus Christ," and that "the words Father, Son, and Holy Ghost were never used in Christian baptism."[40]

This caused a stir in the camp and led several to search the Scriptures that night. Early the next morning, one of them, John G. Scheppe, excitedly awakened people, announcing that the Lord had spoken to him about the need for every true believer to be rebaptized "in the name of Jesus" only.[41] Soon, many noted Assemblies of God leaders were rebaptized in Jesus' name.[42]

To support the "new issue," more "new revelations" were soon put forward. Gregory Boyd explains this development:

> In an attempt to harmonize Matthew 28:19…with the Book of Acts, which, it was thought, always employed the formula 'in the name of Jesus Christ [or 'the Lord Jesus']…certain enthusiastic and uninformed believers in the early Pentecostal movement concluded that the name of the Father, Son, and the Holy Spirit must be Jesus. 'Father,' 'Son,' and 'Holy Spirit,' it was pointed out, are not proper 'names,' but only titles. But 'Jesus' is a proper name and hence must be *the* proper name referred to by all three of these titles….Hence, it was and

is argued, the singular 'name' of the Father, Son, and Holy Spirit is 'Jesus Christ.'[43]

Pentecostal leaders who held to the doctrine of the Trinity gathered to plan to stem the tide of rebaptism. The foremost Trinitarian leader, J. Roswell Flower, succeeded in having the Executive Presbytery call for a General Council to discuss the "New Issue," as the Oneness teaching came to be called. At the third General Council, held in St. Louis, MO, in October 1915, leaders from both camps agreed to table the issue until the next General Council to allow time for more prayer and study. For the time being, the tension was eased, though Carl Brumback calls it "only an armed truce."[44]

The fourth General Council met in St. Louis in October, 1916. Contrary to their 1914 declaration that the Bible was sufficient and no man-made creed was necessary, the Committee on Resolutions proposed a Statement of Fundamental Truths. Despite the protests of the Oneness camp that the resolution was presenting a creed, the majority voted to approve the Statement, which expressed Trinitarian evangelical theology.[45]

The young denomination paid a big price for this final decision. Brumback reports "156 ministers and numerous assemblies missing."[46] Among those who left were a number of founders and leaders of the denomination. Moreover, not all who left were Oneness adherents. Some left because the rejection they had received from their former denominations made them identify with the minority group.[47]

The final decision had another repercussion. The council's decision signaled the distancing of the Assemblies of God from Pentecostals who were prone to new revelations and its adherence to traditional evangelical doctrines. This later opened the way for the group to be accepted in evangelical circles.[48]

Initial Evidence

For a couple of years, there was relative unity and peace among the ranks of the AG. However, in 1918 another issue would disrupt the movement, though without the devastating impact of the 1916 conflict. This time, the AG stand on speaking in tongues as the initial physical evidence of the baptism of the Holy Spirit was called into question.

Central in the conflict was F. F. Bosworth, a much-respected Assemblies of God minister from Canada.[49] Bosworth was a pioneering member of the Assemblies of God and an executive presbyter. This meant that he must have accepted the denomination's Statement of Fundamental Truths.[50] Later, however, Bosworth took note that many who had not spoken in tongues lived exemplary lives and had fruitful and powerful ministries, whereas many of those who claimed to be filled with the Holy Spirit and spoke in tongues lived questionable Christian lives. This led him to conclude that speaking in tongues was only one of the possible evidences that a person had been filled with the Holy Spirit.[51] Many were led to accept Bosworth's stand. Thus, another General Council had to deal with the issue.

On July 24, 1918, Bosworth sent a resignation letter explaining that his resignation was motivated by a desire to save the leadership of the denomination any blame.[52] Although no longer a member, Bosworth attended the General Council in 1918. He was given the opportunity to present his belief, but the body voted that every AG pastor must teach the distinctive doctrine that speaking in tongues must accompany the baptism in the Spirit. Bosworth graciously shook the hands of the other leaders before he departed in peace. Menzies notes that "he took virtually no others with him." Moreover, he maintained fellowship with the Assemblies of God and even cooperated with them in citywide crusades.[53]

Expansion

The organizers of the Assemblies of God in 1914 believed that the cooperative fellowship would be short-lived; their evangelistic thrust would soon usher in Christ's return.[54] Instead, the denomination not only endured but also quickly grew. Despite the internal controversies it faced, its rapid growth was unhampered. The following statistics show the growth of the US Assemblies of God:

Table 1
Growth in the USAG

Year	No. of Ministers[55]	No. of Churches[56]	No. of Members[57]
1916	429	118	6,703
1925	1,155	909	50,386
1941	4,159	4,348	209,549
1961	9,428	8,233	508,602

Moreover, adhering to the Pentecostal theology that the baptism in the Holy Spirit was for enduement of power for witness from Jerusalem to the ends of the earth (Acts 1:8), the Assemblies of God consequently emphasized missions. In fact, as previously stated, one of the reasons for organizing the Assemblies of God was the desire to unite efforts for missions. Secretary of the Assemblies of God John W. Welch was even quoted in the *Pentecostal Evangel* as having said in the 1920 General Council, "The General Council of the Assemblies of God was never meant to be an institution; it is just a missionary agency."[58] It is interesting to note that the first department formally organized by the new denomination was the Missions Department, established in 1919 with J. Roswell Flower appointed as Missionary Secretary.[59] The next Missions Director, Noel Perkin, expounded on what he considered the most important qualification for missionary service: "In considering the objective of missions as the making of disciples and the building of the church, it is important to keep in mind that such ministry can only be effective through the aid and inspiration of God's Spirit. It is a spiritual ministry and can only be carried out by Spirit-filled and God-directed workers. This, therefore, is the primary and most essential qualification. We still need men full of faith and of the Holy Spirit to fulfill this ministry."[60] This statement is still in line with the Assemblies of God theology that Holy Spirit baptism is for enduement of power.

Below are some of the available data illustrating the growth in the missions work of the denomination:

Table 2
Growth of Missions Work in the USAG

Year	Missionaries[61]	World Missions Contribution[62]	Churches and Preaching Pts.[63]	National Ministers[64]	Converts[65]
1917	91	$ 10,223			
1925	250	177,103			
1941	394	573,354			
1952	617	3,406,841	3,897	4,074	252,634
1956	676	4,481,453	13,795	11,338	627,443
1960	784	6,620,857	12,459	12,657	985,241

The missionary zeal of the Assemblies of God led its missionaries to fields where the Pentecostal message had not yet been preached. American Assemblies of God missionaries brought that message to the Philippines in 1926. In 1940, the Philippines District Council of the Assemblies of God was organized.

Chapter 3

Crispulo Garsulao - first Filipino AG pioneer
Source: Asia Pacific Research Center, APTS, Baguio

BACKGROUND AND BIRTH OF THE PGCAG

The Philippines in Esperanza's Lifetime

Dionisio Salazar and Lourdes Ungson have identified three characteristic movements of Asian history: first, pre-colonial days, when Asia was isolated from the Western world; second, Western imperialism in Asia, motivated by trade and commerce and fueled by the Industrial Revolution in Europe; and third, the movement against colonialism, spearheaded by Asian intellectuals and nationalists, that gave way to revolutions.[1]

When Rodrigo Esperanza was born in 1908, the Philippines had already experienced all three movements. Before the turn of the twentieth century, the country had almost achieved freedom from one empire but found itself under the rule of another. After more than 300 years of Spanish rule, the Philippines was ceded by the Spanish crown to the United States in exchange for twenty million dollars[2] at the Treaty of Paris, which ended the Spanish-American War on December 10, 1898.[3] Filipino soldiers, already fighting the Spanish colonizers before the Americans came, now turned their arms against the new invaders. History records this period as the Philippine-American War. In 1902, after three years of fighting, the Philippine army surrendered to the superior military might of the US.[4] Thus, Esperanza was born into a country that was transitioning from the rule of a Spanish Roman Catholic colonizer to that of an American Protestant colonizer.

Some historians aver that US President William McKinley opted to retain the Philippines as a colony in the spirit of the poem, "The White Man's Burden: The United States and the Philippine Islands," written by the famous British novelist and poet, Rudyard Kipling:

> Take up the White Man's burden—
> Send forth the best ye breed—
> Go, bind your sons to exile
> To serve your captives' need;
> To wait, in heavy harness,
> On fluttered folk and wild—
> Your new-caught sullen peoples,
> Half devil and half child.[5]

Speaking to a group of Methodist ministers, President McKinley was reported to have declared, "[T]here was nothing left for us to do but to take them all, and to educate the Filipinos, and uplift and civilize and Christianize them, and by God's grace do the best we could by them, as our fellow-men for whom Christ died."[6] Many Christians, especially American missionaries, believed it was their country's duty to Christianize the Philippines. However, other historians believe that the US President's motive was mostly economic. Antonio Molina asserts that the United States was hoping that the Philippines would give them "an entering wedge for the penetration of Far Eastern trade."[7]

Similar to sentiments against Spanish colonizers in the past, anti-Americanism was now the focus of Filipino nationalists. However, another group of Filipinos saw the Americans as a source of economic, political, and military prosperity.[8] For their part, the Americans realized that winning the military battle was not sufficient to conform Filipinos to the American way of life. They had to contend with the Filipinos' native culture as well as the anti-Protestant attitude of the predominantly Roman Catholic country. Since Americans were generally perceived to be Protestants, Roman Catholic Filipinos were doubly wary of the new colonizers. Thus, while still fighting those considered to be rebels, the American colonizers educated those who had already been pacified.

American values began to infiltrate Filipino culture, and print media started heralding these values. Several newspapers began publication, including *The Bounding Billow, The American Soldier, The Manila Times, The American,* and *The Manila Daily Bulletin.*[9] Yet among all the methods used to re-orient the Filipino mind, the "principal agent of Americanization was the public school system, and the master stroke of educational policy was the adoption of English as the medium of instruction."[10] The fact that the Philippines, at that time, had more schools than many other countries aside from Europe and some colonies of Spain in South and Central America made the public school system the most logical avenue for instilling American values and dreams in Filipinos.[11] To be successful in the re-orientation task, American educators first needed to understand some basic aspects of Filipino culture.

Philippine Culture, Early 1900s

The Filipino culture in the early 1900s was the product of Asian, Spanish, pagan, and Roman Catholic influences.

Filipino Family and Values

As in other countries, the basic Philippine social unit is the family. However, the Filipino family system was, and still is, multilineal, meaning that

> one can trace relationship with anyone in a given community. The relationship may either be by upward descent through the parents or downward through either male or female progeny and their spouses. Sometimes the relationship is also traceable through the siblings. It is not rare, therefore, that one community may be composed of one extended family.[12]

One implication of this system is that the Filipino strives for harmony of relationships. This is expressed through basic Filipino values such as *hiya*, or "shame," which forces a person to take actions or make decisions that avoid embarrassment; *pakikisama*, which forces an individual to go with the flow of the group despite personal inconvenience; and *utang na loob*, a perpetual debt of gratitude for a favor received. All three values tend to make Filipinos subservient, especially when seen in the light of the *padrino* system, in which persons in higher positions give special favors to subordinates close to them.[13]

Filipino Society

At the turn of the twentieth century, the Philippines was a peasant society with agriculture as its main source of livelihood. Over 300 years of Spanish colonial rule had created a wide gap between the small community of rich Spaniards and Spanish *mestizos*, those with mixed Spanish and Filipino native blood, and the vast majority of lower class Filipinos, called the common *tao*, most of whom were farm laborers or employees in the businesses of the elite. The owners were the patrons, taking care of the laborers while the laborers gave loyalty and assistance to the owners, creating a mutually dependent relationship between the two classes.[14]

However, this symbiotic relationship came under increasing tension:

> The late twenties saw a great intensification of unrest and of organizational activity in both the peasant and labor fronts. This was a reflection of steadily deteriorating conditions which would culminate in the depression of the early thirties. The market crash of 1929 brought economic prostration to the Philippines. Prices of the basic export crops dropped drastically, causing grave hardship on the peasantry. Many were evicted from land and home and even those who continued working sank deeper into debt. Urban workers lost their jobs as businesses failed. Others suffered cuts in wages as employers passed on to them part of their reverses....It is therefore not surprising that the late twenties and the thirties were turbulent years.[15]

Filipino Christianity

The centrality of the family in Filipino relationships is manifested even in religion. In the past, many homes had a family shrine which was the center of worship during regular family prayer hours, a symbol of the "family-centeredness" of religious activities in the Filipino home.[16] Melba Maggay calls the form of Christianity that developed in the Philippines a "sandwich religion," because it was "a layer of Christian beliefs piled on top of a largely pagan slice of bread."[17] Moreover, Leonardo Mercado distinguishes three basic kinds of Catholicism practiced in the country: "(1) official Catholicism which is characterized by laws even in worship, (2) so-called 'folk

Catholicism' which consists of tolerated practices beyond the control of the hierarchy, and (3) the practices of 'animistic' religion."[18]

Filipino folk Catholicism's syncretism is illustrated by common beliefs regarding the cause of illness. Michael Tan identifies three basic theories of illness held by Filipinos, which are perpetuated even today:

> **Mystical** theories attribute illness to the automatic consequence of the victim's acts and behavior. **Personalist** theories attribute illnesses to the active intervention of sensate agents such as supernatural entities or malevolent human beings. Finally, **naturalistic** theories attribute illnesses to impersonal natural forces or conditions such as cold, heat, winds or an imbalance of the body's elements.[19]

Interestingly, it is possible for a Filipino to adhere to all three theories. Thus, it is common for a sick Filipino to consult both a medical doctor and a *babaylan* (village medicine man or woman) to heal a particular disease. Maggay explains this specific syncretism:

> [S]ome recognition needs to be made that we are dealing with a culture where anyone speaking for God, be he priest or medium or *babaylan*, is assumed to be a man of power. One is up against the expectation that nearness to God means access to divine resource, a secret pipeline to the source of all power.[20]

Another value that affects Christianity in the Philippines is *hiya*. *Hiya* leads to split-level Christianity:

> which permits the coexistence of two or more systems of thought and behavior simultaneously within the self, the topmost or surface system being that which [was] received from the Christian industrial West and a deeper system, the relics of an ancient culture....*Hiya* forces the individual to conform to the expectations of two semi-opposed groups.[21]

Moreover, since God is perceived as inaccessible or remote, one needs intermediaries to reach him.[22] In the context of the *padrino* system, Mary, the mother of Jesus, and the saints are the favored intermediaries through whom one can present petitions to and obtain answers from God.

Hiya, pakikisama, utang na loob, the *padrino* system, animistic religion, and folk Catholicism were just some of the varied aspects of the Filipino culture that Protestant missionaries had to contend with or even learn to use in their efforts to spread the gospel among the newly-conquered people. Yet there were other factors outside Filipino culture that spurred the American missionaries in the task of converting the locals.

Inroads of Protestantism

Domingo Diel Jr. points to the distribution of Bibles or specific books of the Bible in the Philippines decades before the coming of the Protestant missionaries as one of the factors that paved the way for Protestant work. He believes that the translation of the Bible into the local dialects and the concomitant distribution work of religious book peddlers helped prepare the hearts and minds of the Filipinos to receive the gospel brought by the missionaries and led to the rapid spread of Protestant Christianity, especially in the Western Visayas.[23]

While the Bible was being distributed in the Philippines, halfway around the world, many Americans had begun to desire expansion beyond their continent. Gerald Anderson observes:

> Until the 1890's...Manifest Destiny was thought of primarily in terms of continental expansion, the absorption of North America, with the consent of the people about to be absorbed and with a view toward their admission to citizenship and statehood. In the 1890's, however, when the United States had reached the limits of prospective continental expansion and as the nation's economy reached maturity, there developed considerable agitation for expansion beyond the continent of North America, to permit further growth in the nation's economy, to provide outposts of national defense, and to allow the benevolent spread of American benefits to those less fortunate.[24]

To many American Christians, one of the "American benefits" that needed to be spread was Protestant Christianity. Thus, various mission boards readily made plans to send missionaries to the Philippines when it was acquired by the US.

On July 13, 1898, barely two months after US Navy Commodore George Dewey defeated the Spanish fleet in Manila Bay, the foreign mission boards of the Reformed Church of America, the Congregational Church, the American Baptist Union, the Methodist Episcopal Church, and the Presbyterian Church in the United States of America met and agreed to form a Joint Committee on the Philippine Islands Mission. Each of those denominations appointed two representatives to serve on that Committee.[25] The Committee agreed on plans to send missionaries to the newly-acquired country.

From 1899 to 1902, seven US Protestant missions opened work in the Philippines. The Presbyterians came first with the arrival of James Burton Rodgers in April 1899 as the first regular missionary to the country. The Methodists then sent Thomas H. Martin, who arrived on March 25, 1900. Eric Lund, of the American Baptist Foreign Mission Society, arrived in Iloilo in May 1900. Next came Edwin S. Eby and Sanford B. Kurtz, the first United Brethren missionaries, who arrived on April 1, 1901. The Churches of Christ (Disciples) sent their first missionaries, William H. Hanna and his wife, who arrived in Manila in August 1901. The Congregational Churches were represented by Robert Franklin Black, who arrived in Manila in November 1902 and then proceeded to Mindanao to scout for the best location for his mission work. Although in 1898 Episcopal chaplains accompanied the American troops who came to the Philippines and, thus, were already conducting services among American soldiers and Filipinos, it was not until November 1899 that James Smiley was appointed as the first Episcopal missionary to the Philippines. However, he soon returned home due to an injury. Other missionaries were sent as his replacement.[26]

Evangelism

Evangelism was the primary aim of all the mission boards. For example, in a 1925 conference, representatives of the Northern Baptist Convention's American Baptist Foreign Mission Society and Woman's American Baptist Foreign Mission Society declared that their primary aim was "to lead men everywhere to accept Jesus Christ as Savior and Lord, through whom they may find the Father, and to establish among them New Testament churches to maintain and propagate the teachings of Jesus Christ."[27] Indeed, the goal to "save the heathens" was at the forefront of the Protestant missionaries' hearts, although referring to the Filipinos as "heathen" was generally avoided in missionary records since the majority of the country's population belonged to the Roman Catholic Church, albeit as nominal members.[28]

Education

If evangelism was the primary aim of the missionaries, education and health ministries were among their most important tools for evangelism. For example, Anne Kwantes points to the works of three Presbyterian missionaries who came to the Philippines between April 1899 and October 1900. James B. Rodgers focused on evangelism, J. Andrew Hall on medical care, and David S. Hibbard on Christian education. Rodger's work led to the founding of many Filipino congregations with ordained Filipino Presbyterian clergy. Hall put up a *nipa* hospital and trained Filipino nurses. Under his tutelage, three Filipinas graduated as nurses after a 3-year training program, the first Filipinas to receive training in what was then modern professional nursing.[29] Hibbard's educational zeal led to the establishment of Silliman Institute (now Silliman University), from which three Filipinos graduated in March 1910, one each in law, civil engineering, and clerical studies, the first to receive government-accredited degrees.[30]

Teodoro Agoncillo, a noted Filipino historian, declares that "[T]he greatest contribution of the United States to Philippine civilization is the system of public education."[31] The Americans established seven schools within three months after the Battle of Manila Bay. They then created primary schools and schools for higher education. Moreover, they sent Filipinos with special aptitudes to the US for training. American missionaries first experimented with adult education in non-Christian localities; the program was later continued by state-supported universities.

The literacy campaign also resulted in economic uplift, especially of recently converted Protestant families living in rural areas. With the "Protestant conviction that all their new Christian brothers and sisters were entitled to the best in education, the second generation *barrio* Christians became [professionals]—and moved to town!"[32]

Early American Protestant missionaries who came to the Philippines saw the public school system not only as a principal agent of Americanization, but also as a means to liberate Filipinos from Roman Catholic authority.[33] When asked why they needed to evangelize the Roman Catholic Filipinos, Protestant missionaries acknowledged that the Roman Catholic Church should be credited for introducing basic concepts of Christianity, yet insisted that the Catholic Church was unable to present to the people the terms of salvation, incorporated pagan rituals into its own worship, failed to combat superstition, and failed to relate religion to the living of a moral life.[34]

However, efforts to set Filipinos free from Roman Catholic influence were resisted by some locals. Frank Laubach dedicates a whole chapter in one of his books to the persecution that many Filipino Protestant laity suffered at the hands of fiercely loyal Roman Catholics.[35] Nevertheless, Protestant churches continued to show remarkable growth. By 1954, Protestant churches numbered 1,713 with 195,245 members. Averell Aragon observes that based on the above figures, in the fifty-five year span from 1899 to 1954, the Protestants won 3,315 converts and established 31 churches per year, this at a period when Protestantism was new and still acculturating in the country.[36]

Health Ministries

Among all of the United States' contributions to the Philippines, Agoncillo ranks its scientific program of public health and welfare second in importance. America's health program greatly reduced the incidence of deadly diseases such as cholera, smallpox, dysentery, malaria, and tuberculosis. Moreover, it stopped the spread of epidemics brought in from other countries. This was accomplished by facing the "formidable wall of ignorance and superstition" of the Filipinos that made them more susceptible to these diseases.[37] The vital role of medical missionaries in missions cannot be overestimated. The ministry of medical missionaries like Hibbard met a real need among Filipinos mostly adhering to animistic religion or folk Catholicism. The missionaries' ability to heal earned them the people's respect. The inherent *utang na loob* of those who had been healed made them willing to grant their "healers" the opportunity to share the gospel. Indeed, Andrew Walls emphasizes the fact that medical missionaries both aided missionary health and efficiency and also provided a hearing for missions when no other form of mission work was successful.[38]

The hard work of American missionaries, educators, and health workers was well rewarded. Nick Joaquin, the 1976 Filipino National Artist awardee, writes that through the 1920s, Filipinos increasingly thought of themselves as being "almost American."[39] Despite the disparity between the treatment given to Americans and that given to Filipinos in their own country, Joaquin writes that the "myth of perfect understanding, perfect communion, had become so established nothing could disturb it, not even the glaring fact that the two peoples living side by side were not even, socially, on speaking terms."[40] Even in churches, "the bulk of the congregation remained loyal, and a fascination with America was a notable attribute of prominent Filipino Protestant clergymen."[41]

Inroads of Pentecostalism

Being a relatively young movement, Pentecostalism's missions programs had just started and many of their missionaries went to the mission field "by faith." The Mission Board of the Church of God (COG), in Cleveland, Tennessee reports:

> In the early years of Pentecost, many people were wont to sell their possessions and launch out into a mission field entirely on faith, without promise of backing or support. The Lord has honored this in many cases where He has distinctly ordered it, and to His great glory. But experience shows that in the greater number of cases this kind of action has produced much suffering and hardship....[42]

Too soon, some missionary pioneers had to return to their homeland, leaving behind a ministry in its infant stage. In the Philippines, similar instances were recorded, but Filipino pastors stepped in to fill the gap when American missionaries left.

Reports from three Pentecostal groups originating in the US around the time that Rodrigo Esperanza was becoming involved in the fledgling movement reflect the work of Filipino Pentecostal pioneers in the Philippines. In 1947, the COG sent Frank Parado as their first missionary to the country. Conn records:

> Parado remained in the Philippine Islands only about eighteen months. When he returned to the States, he appointed Fulgencio R. Cortez, an Ilocano Christian in the northeastern province of Catagayan [sic], to care for the churches in his absence. Under the leadership of

Cortez and other Filipino workers, a fruitful program of evangelism was begun.[43]

The Filipino workers, whether or not under the leadership of American missionaries, did not balk at opposition and hardship in their pioneering work. Conn describes the COG pioneers' efforts: "They pressed into remote villages of the northern provinces of Luzon, carrying their musical instruments and Bibles with them, building brush arbors, talking to those they met, regularly winning souls to Christ."[44]

American Protestant Missionaries' Role in the Colonial Government

It cannot be denied that the Filipinos' nationalistic pride, which had risen against the Spaniards, found similar expression against the American Protestant missionaries, who were perceived to have played a crucial role in the American colonial program and greatly contributed to its advancement.[45] For example, the early American Protestant missionaries followed the American government's thrust and likewise used education as an agent of civilization, aiding in making many Filipinos think of themselves as "almost American."

Lamin Sanneh, however, sees another aspect of the missionaries' work. Specifically focusing on Bible translations, he avows that instead of missions serving as a tool of imperialism and civilization, the missionaries' efforts to translate Christianity into the local culture and dialect were indigenization in the best sense.[46] He observes that missionary linguistic research and translations stimulated cultural pride. Viewed in this context, missions helped provide nationalism with the resources it needed to flower and flourish.[47]

Moreover, Kenton Clymer points out that many early Protestant missionaries in the Philippines sought to shield Filipino indigenous culture from "Western religious and intellectual dominance."[48] They saw the "corrupting, debilitating aspects of advancing 'civilization'" on the local people. They saw the need not only to evangelize the Filipinos but also to protect them by elevating "the spiritual and moral qualities of the American population in the islands."[49]

Thus, after World War II, despite the fact that the Philippine denominations still depended on the US mother denominations for the great bulk of their financial support, Protestant churches began the process of transferring leadership into Filipino hands, albeit with some measure of "missionary initiative and direction."[50]

The Beginnings of the PGCAG

Ma confirms the role of Filipino nationals in the pioneering and expansion efforts of the Assemblies of God in the Philippines. He points out that although Benjamin and Cordelia Caudle were the first Assemblies of God (AG) missionaries to the country, they left after a few years without establishing their work. Later, Filipinos succeeded in establishing the AG work in the Philippines.[51] Trinidad C. Esperanza (younger sister of Rudy Esperanza), in her masters thesis, "The Assemblies of God in the Philippines," the first history of the PGCAG written in an academic setting, concurs with Ma. She writes that since the Caudles left without an established ministry, the AG work in the Philippines was not started by foreign missionaries but by Filipinos who had been converted in the United States and then returned to their hometowns in the Philippines to share the Pentecostal message. Her thesis covers twenty-five years of the PGCAG's history, beginning with the formation of the

Philippines District Council of the Assemblies of God (PDCAG) in 1940 as a district of the Assemblies of God in the US.

Clearly, the growth of early Pentecostal denominations in the Philippines was accomplished in great measure through the efforts of local pioneers.

First USAG Missionaries

The first USAG missionaries to the Philippines, Benjamin and Cordelia Caudle, with their son and two daughters, arrived in Manila in September 1926.[52] They rented a house in Leveriza Street, Malate. Although many Filipinos spoke English by then, Mr. Caudle studied Spanish and Tagalog to communicate better with the people. Mr. Caudle distributed tracts and sold copies of the *Pentecostal Evangel* to open opportunities for sharing the gospel.[53] He also held market and street meetings. Once a week, he invited some young men from local high schools and the University of the Philippines for a Bible study. The couple also conducted a Sunday School in their backyard and at one point had fifty-five attendees, mostly children. Unfortunately, the hot tropical weather proved too much for Mrs. Caudle. She became ill and the couple had to return to the US without anyone taking over the work they had started.[54]

First Filipino AG Pioneer

Before the Caudles left for the US, a young Filipino who had recently graduated from Glad Tidings Bible Institute (later Bethany University), an Assemblies of God Bible school in San Francisco, USA, returned to the Philippines to bring the Pentecostal message to his hometown.

Crispulo Garsulao was among the young men who went to the US seeking greener pastures.[55] His academic achievement as the first civil engineer of the province of Antique had qualified him to be one of the *pensionados* sent to the US for further studies in engineering, receiving a living allowance but no salary.[56] He was converted when he heard the gospel in a street meeting, and he left the university and went to Bible school instead.[57] In 1927, when he graduated from Glad Tidings Bible Institute, he decided to return home and bring the gospel to his own people. He sailed back to the Philippines, leaving the US on February 3, 1928.[58] He later reported that when he landed in Manila, he looked up the Caudles and fellowshipped with them before proceeding home to Villar, Sibalom, Antique.[59]

Garsulao reached his hometown on March 9, 1928.[60] He immediately started evangelizing, beginning with his own family. After their conversion, they became core workers in his newly established church.[61] He reported that some people persecuted the work but others were saved, baptized in water and the Spirit, and healed. The miraculous healings attracted people to the Pentecostal message, and the church started to grow. In his third year of pioneering, he opened the family's house in Sibalom, the town proper, as a Bible training school so he could train workers for the ministry. Initially he had ten students, eight females and two males. Others wanted to join the training, but he could not accommodate them due to lack of space and finances.[62]

Garsulao went back to the US in 1932 to raise funds for a tent he hoped to use for his crusades. He returned to Antique in 1933 and continued the evangelistic thrust. Tragedy struck the pioneering work that year. The Sibalom house used as a Bible training center burned down when an alcohol lamp his brother was refilling exploded. His brother died in that explosion. Still Garsulao pressed on with his pioneering work.[63]

The March 1934 issue of *Glad Tidings* reported that Garsulao had contracted malaria fever but was "on the road to recovery."[64]

However, his hectic schedule lowered his resistance. Once again he fell ill with what the family presumed to be typhoid fever. In the absence of medical personnel and medical facilities in the barrio, the family resorted to homemade concoctions and herbal medicine.[65] Despite his family's efforts, his fever worsened. The March 1935 issue of *Glad Tidings* announced the death of Garsulao on December 17, 1934.[66]

Garsulao's death shook the faith of some of his members, but his female students continued their pioneering work. Soon other pioneers came to help. By 1935, other Filipino Pentecostal ministers in the US had also decided to return to the Philippines and preach their message. The *Intercom*, the official publication of the PGCAG in the early 1990s, lists some of the said pioneers:

> Vision for the lost in his homeland impelled Pedro Collado to leave the States in March 1935 and preached [sic] to his family in Bagumbayan, Nueva Ecija. Then he left them and went to Antique to pastor the flock left behind by Cris Garsulao. Subsequently, Collado followed his people in Pikit, Cotabato, then to Marbel, Koronadal. In November, 1935, Benito P. Acena left San Francisco, California, USA and on New Year's Day 1936 began work in La Paz, Laoag, Ilocos Norte. He established a Pentecostal church there. Rosendo Alcantara later joined Acena in Ilocos Norte where he built a church in Bangay, Dingras[,] Ilocos Norte. Eugenio M. Suede built the first Assemblies of God church in the province of Iloilo. Pedro Castro from Santa Maria, Ilocos Sur had an almost apostolic ministry among the mountain people of Ilocos Sur and Abra. He pioneered the many established churches in the interior towns. Jose Maypa had many places in Capiz. Lorenzo Sebastian preached in Bilad, Camiling, Tarlac. [Cirilo] Barcena began work in Ilagan,

Isabela. Pangasinan province has had several native missionaries from the United States also. Hermogenes Abrenica began a work in San Nicolas, Villasis; Rodrigo Esperanza in Rosario, Pozorrubio; [Servillano] Obaldo in Caramutan, Villasis; and Marcelino Etrata in San Felipe, Binalonan. All of these Filipinos began their work independently of one another.[67]

Of the thirteen pioneers named above, eight were from northern Luzon, while only three were from the Visayas, two from central Luzon, and none from Tagalog-speaking areas. This trend would continue and would later affect the direction of the expansion of the work of the PGCAG. Since most of the early leaders were Ilocanos, more pioneering churches were established in the Ilocano-speaking areas, whether in Luzon or in the settled areas of Mindanao. Being the majority in the denomination in those early years, the needs of the Ilocano-speaking churches were addressed more readily than those of churches in the Visayas and other regions of the country. Yet though in the beginning the pioneers were working independently of one another, conditions soon necessitated that these ministers come together to form an organization.

The Philippines District Council of the Assemblies of God

In those pioneering days, the Philippines was still a protectorate of the United States. US policy was that a denomination must register with the US Consul General in Manila before it could operate in the Philippines. Moreover, the denomination's head in the country must be a missionary or church leader appointed by the home body in the US.[68] The Filipino Pentecostal ministers' churches, which lacked government recognition, were considered to be cults. This made them subject to persecution both from the Roman Catholics and from the evangelicals. Pentecostal ministers needed official recognition to avail of legal protection, rights, and privileges, such as the authority to solemnize marriages. Moreover, they recognized "a need of stabilizing fellowship, establishing standards for doctrine and practice and the organization of the churches for a united effort in the propagation of the Pentecostal message."[69]

Meanwhile, in the US, Rodrigo Esperanza graduated from Northwest Bible Institute and planned to go back to the Philippines to start work in the name of the Assemblies of God. He found that many Filipino Pentecostals who had returned to that country had joined either the Filipino Assemblies of the First-Born, the Foursquare Church, or the Church of God. He and Rev. E[steban] C. Lagmay, President of the organization of Filipino Assemblies of God ministers in the US, presented their request to the USAG that a missionary be sent to the Philippines to organize the Assemblies of God there. He later learned that Leland and Helen Johnson had already been appointed to the task.[70]

Esperanza arrived in the Philippines on May 9, 1939. He immediately started evangelistic work in Pozorrubio, Pangasinan, his hometown. He also contacted other Filipino pastors and pioneers who were uncommitted to any denomination and invited them to come to an organizational convention of the Assemblies of God. The Johnsons and their children arrived in the Philippines on Christmas Eve, 1939. The following month, Johnson, Esperanza, Rosendo Alcantara, and Hermogenes Abrenica made plans for the convention.[71]

At Abrenica's invitation, the convention was held at his church in San Nicolas, Villasis, Pangasinan on March 21-27, 1940. At the request of the USAG, Glenn Dunn also attended the convention to aid the Johnsons in organizing the group. He was an AG missionary assigned to South China and was on his way to the USA for furlough.[72] Johnson showed the pastors the legal papers given him by the USAG Foreign Missions Department in order to register in the Philippines a District Council of the USAG and file the organization's charter with the Philippine government.[73]

The convention was spent in inspirational services, worship, and fellowship, followed by the election of officers. Aside from Johnson, who was appointed by the mother organization in the US, the following were elected as executive officers:

Superintendent	Leland Johnson
Secretary	Rodrigo Esperanza
Treasurer	Pedro Castro
General Presbyters	Rosendo Alcantara, Hermogenes Abrenica[74]

The body also decided on the following sectional divisions for the country:

Section 1	Ilocos Norte and Cagayan Valley
Section 2	Ilocos Sur and Abra
Section 3	La Union and Mountain Province
Section 4	Pangasinan to Albay and Sorsogon
Section 5	Eastern Visayas Islands
Section 6	Western Visayas and Islands
Section 7	Mindanao and Islands[75]

The Philippines District Council of the Assemblies of God (PDCAG) was duly registered at the Philippine Securities and Exchange Commission on July 11, 1940.[76]

War Years

Hardly had the newly organized group taken off when the Philippines became one of the battlegrounds of World War II. Agoncillo succinctly describes those years in the Philippines:

> ...[T]he Japanese, looking for territories to accommodate not only their excess population but also their manufactured goods, started the war in the Pacific. Japanese naval bombers attacked Pearl Harbor in Hawaii in December 1941. The United States declared war against Japan and the war in the Pacific was formally on. As a consequence of this war, the Philippines was occupied by the Japanese. For three years the Filipinos suffered the rigors of war. Civil liberties were suppressed by the enemy, the economy was geared to the demands of the Japanese war efforts, education was revamped to re-orient Filipino thinking along Japanese lines, and political life was limited to the Japanese-sponsored Republic. Meanwhile, thousands upon thousands were executed and imprisoned, but the spirit of revolt continued to plague Japanese authorities to the end of the occupation.[77]

The long wait [for liberation] ended when American forces hit the beach of Leyte in October 1944. Other landings were made in Mindoro, Batangas, and Lingayen in subsequent months. On Feb. 3, 1945, elements of the American army entered Manila. Pursuit of the enemy followed. On August 15, Japan surrendered, and on September 2 the terms of surrender were signed on the battleship *Missouri* at Tokyo Bay. The war in the Pacific was over.[78]

Along with other Protestant missionaries, the Johnson family as well as other AG missionaries from China who had come to help in the work in the Philippines, were all taken prisoner and held for the duration of the war. In the absence of the missionaries, Esperanza and Alcantara served as General Overseers of the young denomination. Alcantara brought food to the starving missionaries in the concentration camps whenever possible. The pastors also continued preaching, although their sermons were screened by the Intelligence Office of the Japanese Imperial Army. To the Filipino pastors was left the task of ministering to their flocks suffering under the repressive Japanese regime.[79]

Post-War Growth

Immediately after the war, the interned American AG missionaries were repatriated to the United States. Meanwhile, the Filipinos lost no time in continuing where the PDCAG had left off when the war interrupted its plans. In the absence of a duly appointed Superintendent, Esperanza requested temporary appointment to the position. On behalf of the USAG Foreign Missions Department, Noel Perkin, Missionary Secretary, sent the needed appointment.[80] Esperanza served as Acting Superintendent and at the same time retained his post as Secretary of the PDCAG.[81]

Soon many USAG missionaries came to the Philippines and the denomination experienced rapid growth. Ma gives the following list of missionaries and their areas of ministry: church pioneers were Elva Vanderbout in the Mountain Province, Warren Denton in Antique, Gunder Olsen in Iloilo City, and Calvin Zeissler in Bacolod City; Edwin Brengle helped establish Immanuel Bible Institute (IBI) in Leyte and Cebu; Paul Pipkin pioneered in Manila with the help of other former missionaries;

Floyd Horst established Evangel Printing Press in Manila; Glenn Dunn headed Bethel Bible Institute (BBI) in Manila and established the Assemblies of God Bible Institute of Mindanao (AGBIM); and Mayme Williams did evangelistic work throughout the archipelago. Aside from Williams, Ma likewise notes the contribution of the following visiting evangelists: Harvey McAlister, A. C. Valdez, Clifton Erickson, Oral Roberts, Rudy Cerullo, T. L. Osborn, Hal Herman, and Ralph Byrd.[82]

The Philippines General Council of the Assemblies of God

On Wednesday, April 21, during the 1953 PDCAG annual convention, the following resolution was presented by the Resolution Committee and unanimously accepted by the whole body:

> Whereas the works in the Philippines have grown in all the archipelago which require more time, more money, and more efforts for supervision from the office of the District Superintendent, and,
> Whereas the works in every geographical division necessitates extra effort, time, money for proper supervision, and,
> Whereas the whole work in general should be a unit organization; Be it therefore resolved that this body, the Philippines District Council of the Assemblies of God in session amend (turn) the present District Council into a General Council creating as many districts as deemed necessary and approved by the General Council.[83]

Elected executive officers were the following:

General Superintendent	R. C. Esperanza
Asst. Gen. Superintendent	Jose Maypa
General Secretary	S. M. Obaldo
General Treasurer	C. Barcena
General Presbyters	B. Maningan, Glenn Dunn, P. Masuecos

This time, the country was divided into 3 districts: Luzon, Visayas, and Mindanao. The Philippines General Council of the Assemblies of God (PGCAG) was duly registered with the Philippine Securities and Exchange Commission on September 23, 1953.[84]

Further Growth and Expansion

After its separation from the USAG as an independent entity, the PGCAG continued to multiply its membership. Major cities in Luzon, Visayas, and Mindanao were penetrated in the 1950s.[85]

In Manila, a rather unusual situation that aided the growth of the PGCAG was the development of a symbiotic relationship between the PGCAG and the Methodist Church in Taytay, Rizal.[86] In 1953, through a journalist's error, Lester Sumrall, a missionary of the USAG, was identified as a Methodist minister when a picture of him praying for a demon-possessed girl appeared in the *Manila Times*. Ruben Candelaria, Superintendent of the Manila District of the Methodist Church in the Philippines at that time, looked for this Methodist missionary ministering in his district without his knowledge. The meeting of the two ministers led to a close friendship. When Candelaria introduced Sumrall to his cousin, David Candelaria, pastor of the Taytay

Methodist Church, a friendship likewise developed between Sumrall and his cousin. This led to the participation of the Taytay Methodist Church in many activities of the AG in Manila.[87] They even helped raise funds for the construction of Bethel Temple in Manila.

When Ralph Byrd conducted crusades in Manila in 1955 and introduced the baptism of the Holy Spirit accompanied by speaking in tongues, the two Methodist pastors were ushered into the Pentecostal experience, "that is the baptism in the Holy Spirit with speaking in tongues as it was in Acts 2:4."[88] Up to this time, speaking in tongues as the initial physical evidence of the baptism in the Holy Spirit was not yet taught among Filipino AG churches, although many AG members spoke in tongues. It seems that Esperanza did not write about speaking in tongues. Instead, his writings emphasize salvation, healing, the second coming, and the empowering of the Holy Spirit without mentioning the doctrine of speaking in tongues as "initial physical evidence." The early teachings of the Filipino AG support Allan Anderson's stand that describing Pentecostalism using the "four-fold pattern," which includes *glossolalia* as the initial physical evidence of the baptism in the Holy Spirit, "can only be neatly applied to 'classical Pentecostalism' in North America."[89]

Through the ministry of Ernie Reb, another USAG missionary, most of Taytay Methodist Church's congregation embraced the Pentecostal experience and the AG doctrine of Christ as Savior, Baptizer, Physician, and soon coming King. Inevitably, this led to a split in the church, with the majority of the congregation holding to their Pentecostal experience. With David Candelaria, this group formed the Taytay Methodist Community Church (TMCC).

TMCC never joined the PGCAG but maintained a friendly relationship with the denomination. Young people from the church and its daughter churches studied at BBI, and some of them later became ministers of the PGCAG. Foremost among these young people was Eleazer Javier, who, after graduating from BBI, was released by his mother church and became a pastor of Bethel Temple in Manila. He soon rose in the PGCAG ranks and became General Superintendent of the denomination, serving from 1977 to 1997.[90]

Meanwhile, the Candelarias' influence in helping bring Pentecostalism into the Methodist Church is supported by the denomination's records. The Methodist Church's 1955 to 1961 statistics show that more than 600 members of Ruben's erstwhile district, the Manila District, transferred to Pentecostal churches.[91]

Continued Growth Into the Twenty-First Century

Two major conflicts, the split of Manila Bethel Temple in 1965 and the split of the denomination in the 1970s, hampered the phenomenal growth of the Assemblies of God. Another group separated from the PGCAG in 1980.[92] Montgomery and McGavran report that the denomination lost momentum during those conflicts, "plummeting from 278 percent to 81 percent DGR (decadal growth rate) for new members and 74 percent to 29 percent DGR for new churches" between 1974 and 1978. The group continued to grow, although at a much slower pace.[93]

The PGCAG commissioned its first Filipino cross-cultural missionaries in 1973. Rev. and Mrs. Cres and Norma Fernandez with their three children were sent to Vietnam. They were precursors of the PGCAG's active involvement as a missions-sending body.[94]

Ma brings the PGCAG story to the close of the twentieth century:

> According to statistics available in 1999, there were 2,357 local churches (almost twice the 1979 [sic] number) with close to 130,000 members, as well as 3,200 affiliated ministers/workers. The Philippine AG also has 35 ministerial training schools (including one for the deaf) and has trained and sent 15 cross-cultural missionaries overseas.[95]

At the DAWN Congress, in September 2001, statistics showed that the PGCAG had the largest number of congregations with 2,853.[96] A vigorous church-planting program called Summer of Service (SOS), the brain child of PGCAG General Superintendent Rev. Reynaldo Calusay when he was the Senior Pastor of First Assembly of God in Roxas City, uses the principle of mobilization of members. Since its launching in 1986, the program has planted more than a hundred churches nationwide.[97] The Executive Leadership is currently collating data to get more updated figures.[98]

This successful and steady growth would not have been possible without the work of the early pioneers discussed in this chapter. Foremost in influence among the PGCAG pioneers is Rudy Esperanza. Let us look at his formative years to see how God shaped him to be the great and influential leader that he was.

Chapter 4

The Rodrigo Esperanza family: Rudy, Leonor, Rudy Jr.
Rebecca, Lydia, and Daniel
Source: Lydia Esperanza Javier

ESPERANZA'S BACKGROUND

Formative Years

Reverend Rodrigo "Rudy" C. Esperanza was one of the most influential Filipino AG pioneers. This chapter traces his formative years, describing his birth and family background, his childhood experiences from preschool to student years, and his personal ambitions that led him to the US where he was saved and received a call to the ministry. There were various factors in Esperanza's background and upbringing that helped mold his character and vision and made him a truly influential person.

Family Background

Rudy Esperanza was born on April 20, 1908, to a Roman Catholic family.[1] He was the eldest child of Dionisio Esperanza and Saturnina Cabanilla Esperanza, both of Ilocos Sur, who had become farmers in the barrio of Rosario, Pozorrubio,

Pangasinan.² He had three sisters: Trinidad, Juanita, and Julia; and three brothers: Rufino, Emiliano, and Ernesto.³

Rudy's mother went through difficult labor when he was born. In accordance with the community's belief at that time, his father was made to crawl down the stairs of their house and then turn around to aid the baby in coming out of the womb.⁴ The practice was believed to have worked, because Rudy came out healthy. In fact, he started walking when he was only seven months old.

Childhood Experiences[5]

Many stories from Rudy's childhood show that he manifested a courageous and adventurous spirit while growing up.

Preschool Years

When Rudy was four years old, a noontime fire burned down several homes in their barrio. His parents searched for him in vain and were overcome with grief, believing that he had died in the fire. Around 4:00 p.m., they heard someone running through the tall cogon grass. To their great relief, they discovered it was Rudy. Somehow, at that young age, he was able to escape the fire and get home four hours later.

Filipino farming communities are commonly laid out with the homes clustered in the center of the barrio or town and the farm fields lying on the outskirts of the community. Rudy's barrio had this layout. Thus, Rudy's father farmed a field about two kilometers away from their home. One morning, at 4 a.m., Dionisio headed for the farm for plowing. Upon reaching his field, he sensed something following him. Thinking it was a dog, he turned around to drive it away. Instead, he saw four-year-old Rudy. The account does not explain why Rudy followed his father to the field, but it must have taken a lot of mettle for a prekindergarten boy to wake up that early and walk two kilometers in the darkness behind his unknowing father.

By age five, Rudy was already tending *carabaos* (water buffaloes), cows, and horses in the pasture. Being quite small, he would make his *carabao* lie down so that he could climb on its back. Once, his *carabao* got into a fight with another *carabao*. Since he could not dismount, he stayed on top of his *carabao* until the end of the fight. Upon reaching home, he excitedly recounted his experience. Obviously he did not think of the possibility that he could have been hurt. He was more focused on the thrill of the experience.

Rudy loved following his father around and even shared his passion for hunting. While they were hunting in a forest ten kilometers away from their house, a wild pig rushed past Rudy. He was frightened but still had the presence of mind to scramble up a big rock and shout to the other hunters to come and chase the pig.

Student Days

When Rudy turned six, his father enrolled him in the primary school in their barrio. However, when examination time came, he was not allowed to take the test because he was under-aged. Despite this, he was chosen as "Best Gardener" of the class and received a hoe for his prize. That award was only the beginning. At the end of each school year, Rudy would bring home various honors and awards. Early in life, Rudy distinguished himself in academics.

After five years in primary school, Rudy was sent to the town proper for further schooling. Pozorrubio was five kilometers away, so he stayed in the town on school days and came home on Saturdays to help in the farm work, plowing the field and taking care of the *carabao*. At age fourteen, he went to the high school in Lingayen, the capital of Pangasinan. This time he stayed in a boarding house with other relatives. He studied for four years in Pangasinan High School.[6]

Rudy learned the value of fulfilling duties and responsibilities as a young boy. Moreover, the school days spent away from home developed in him an independent spirit. Thus, after high school, when tragedy struck the family and his mother passed away after two years of lingering sickness, Rudy had the courage to leave home and seek his fortune in the US.

Journey to the US

After World War I, America needed laborers and sought to attract Filipino hired hands. Many advertisements depicted the advantages of living in the US. Moreover, steamship companies told stories of America's "streets strewn with gold." On top of this, American textbooks used by American teachers described the greatness of the US. Thus, many high school graduates dreamed of going to America to study as self-supporting students.[7]

Like many other Filipino youth, Rudy grew up longing to see the American "Mainland."[8] He, like Garsulao, desired to seek his fortune in the US. He was inspired by shipping agents' stories about self-supporting Filipinos who studied in America and became successful in their careers. After finishing high school, he took the Civil Service examination, but the exam result was delayed. He took this to mean that he had failed. Thus, he decided to pursue his dream and seek his fortune in America. Barely eighteen years old, he left on board the RMS Empress of Asia, bound for Seattle, Washington. His father provided him with some funds to buy the ticket. About the time he reached Japan, his father received the result of his Civil Service examination. He had passed and was offered a job as *Delegado Provincial* (Chief Clerk), but the offer came too late.[9]

Conversion and Call to the Ministry[10]

As returning Filipino pastors often said in those early days, they went to the US to seek gold, instead, they found God.[11]

Conversion

Rudy admitted that when he went to the US, he was running away from God's demands on his life. Although he was born in a Roman Catholic family, Rudy began attending the Methodist church in his hometown before he reached high school. He was actively involved in church activities and went with the Methodist pastor to various outstations where the pastor preached or held Bible studies.[12] After graduation, Rudy was offered a scholarship to a Methodist seminary. However, his youthful plans and ambitions were strong. He turned down the offer and instead headed for America to study and establish a career.[13] He vowed that he would have a large share of what the world had to offer. He promised his father, "I will not come back without an addindum [sic] to my name or a shingle to put outside my window."

When Rudy arrived at the port in Seattle, he was met by a man who drove him straight to a church where a service was ongoing. That man was instrumental in Rudy's landing a job in a salmon cannery in Alaska. The first year in Alaska went well, and he sent all his earnings back home to his father. However, crisis after crisis confronted him the following year: he had an accident in Alaska and lost his job; he received news of the death of an immediate relative, which left him shaken; and lastly, he was caught in the midst of the Great Depression in the US.

After his work in Alaska, Rudy worked as a houseboy in Portland, Oregon, then in a factory in Seattle.[14] He drifted along with other jobseekers in Seattle's Chinatown, each day forgetting more of the things he had learned in Sunday school. He soon imbibed the spirit of the times and in his disillusionment turned from faith to reason.

Looking back, Rudy declared, "In the midst of all these, I found the Lord merciful." He landed a job on a dairy farm in Washington, testing, weighing, and sampling milk and cream.[15] Soon he received a promotion. With his increased income came a greater predilection for the night life. He drifted farther away from God.

One day, Rudy got sick and had to find somebody to take his place at the dairy. He saw a Filipino emerging from the Full Gospel Rescue Mission in Seattle. Believing this to be a good man since he came from a Christian center, he asked the man to substitute for him. The man, Eugenio Almerol, gladly took the job. After work, Almerol went back to Rudy to invite him to attend the service at the Rescue Mission. Rudy waved aside the invitation, pointing to the modernist, evolutionist, and communist books on his table. "Look, I believe in evolution and Jesus was a bastard and the Virgin Mary was a harlot...The first lie is the belief that there is a God," he declared. Yet despite these declarations, deep in his heart, Rudy believed that God existed.

Almerol was persistent. With tears flowing down his face, he earnestly prayed for Rudy. This moved Rudy to attend the service with him. However, Rudy sat in the last row at the back and was out of the Rescue Mission as soon as the service was over. By the time the preacher reached the door to shake his hand, he was already halfway down the block.

The next night, Rudy was back, this time taking courage to sit in the middle row. The speaker was an elderly man named

Fritz Peterson. As Peterson expounded Romans 12:1-2, Rudy became extremely uncomfortable. He wondered how the speaker had learned about his life. He felt that God's Spirit was speaking directly to him. He began to shake like a leaf, sensing God warning him that if he would not give his life—body and soul—to the Lord that night, it would be his last. He held on to the bench in front of him, but he shook all the more. As soon as the preacher finished his message, Rudy rushed to the altar. He testified that as soon as his knees hit the floor, he knew he was forgiven.[16]

Call to the Ministry

After his conversion experience, Rudy's struggles were far from over. He had the impression that God wanted him to consecrate his life to the ministry. However, two things kept Rudy from obeying. First was his own ambition. He wanted to be a self-made man with "a little business, a little house, with a little wife and a little family." Second were memories of conversations with his Methodist pastor in Pangasinan, a young man like himself. As they had walked to the various outstations and preaching points, the pastor would unburden himself to Rudy about the financial difficulties of the ministry. Rudy was so moved with compassion, he promised the Lord that if He would grant his ambitions, Rudy would support seven Methodist pastors. However, he did not want to be one of those poor pastors himself.

Yet he felt the conviction that the Lord wanted him in the ministry. The Lord's call came stronger and stronger. Rudy would say, "Yes," while in the prayer room, but he would waver as soon as he left. The breaking point came during one Sunday morning worship service, while the worship leader was leading in singing this song:

> Though the way seems straight and narrow,
> All I claim was swept away.
> My ambitions, plans and wishes,
> At my feet in ashes lay.

Finally, Rudy surrendered his own ambitions, plans, and wishes. From then on, he saw God's blessings poured out on him. He received the baptism of the Holy Spirit. His love for his own people grew and intensified. He wept for the souls of Filipinos around him.

That burden in his heart opened doors for ministering to Filipinos in Seattle. In 1934, he helped to open a Mission Hall for Filipinos in Chinatown and a Christian Filipino Home, also in Seattle.[17] In his own words, "During these years of taking charge of the Mission and the Home I had proven God to be faithful always at His word and my faith in His promises developed." Believing that he was called to the ministry, he prepared himself by enrolling at Northwest Bible Institute (now Northwest University), a Pentecostal Bible school.

The Filipino Full Gospel Mission Rudy supervised was aided by various Pentecostal groups. Thus, later he could not decide which Pentecostal group to join. The decisive moment came one day in late 1937. While praying for guidance, he sensed God's Spirit saying to him, "If you will be faithful to ME, I will make you someday a delegate of an international convention of the Assemblies of God at Springfield, Missouri."[18] He took this to mean that God wanted him to join the Assemblies of God. He did, and twenty-five years later, he was a delegate of the PGCAG to the AG convention in Springfield, Missouri. By then he was the General Superintendent of the denomination. He wrote, "You cannot possibly imagine the joy, amazement, the impact of the truth of God's word to me as I sat there at Springfield. . . ."

Indeed, the American influence in the Philippines had a strong impact on Rudy's ambitions. The American books he read in school, plus the stories he heard from shipping agents, all fed his dream to study and work in the "Mainland." This pushed him to leave the comfort of his own country at the young age of eighteen and seek his fortune halfway around the globe. Little did he know what great adventures awaited him. God took hold of Rudy's life and gave him a higher goal; the goal of preaching the gospel to his people and winning them to God's kingdom.

Chapter 5

Taken in front of Manila Bethel Temple with Maynard Ketcham, the USAG's Field Secretary for the Far East in the 1960s.
Source: Esperanza Collection, Asia Pacific Research Center, APTS, Baguio City

FOUNDATIONAL ROLES IN THE PGCAG

Those who give birth to a work inevitably set the vision and mission that will guide the accomplishment of the tasks on which a group embarks. For the Assemblies of God's work in the Philippines, the Filipino pioneers were the guides who set the purpose of the new denomination, a purpose that is now enshrined in their Constitution's preamble. The ministries of these pioneers modeled those priorities before the younger generation, demonstrating how and where things were to be done. Moreover, the pioneers' lives modeled the character required of leaders of the new group.

As the first Filipino holding the highest leadership position open to a national in the denomination, Rodrigo Esperanza had the distinct opportunity to mold the goal and vision of the PDCAG/PGCAG and influence the decisions the new Pentecostal group made as it took its first steps in spreading the Pentecostal message across the Philippine archipelago. Among the Filipino ministers who had come to pioneer the Pentecostal work in their country, Esperanza's high-profile leadership position made him a prominent example for the rest to emulate and/or scrutinize.

This chapter and the subsequent chapters will deal with Esperanza's leadership roles and the leadership character he manifested that left an imprint in the lives of other AG ministers in particular and the PGCAG in general.

Organizer[1]

As shown in a previous chapter, Esperanza played a major role in organizing the Assemblies of God denomination in the Philippines. There were other Pentecostal denominations that he could have joined, but he felt that God clearly gave him a promise if he would join the Assemblies of God. This was significant in view of the fact that the Filipino Mission Hall he organized in 1934 was established with the help of the Filipino Assemblies of the First-Born (FAFB), a non-AG organization ministering in California that had been founded in the early 1930s to give Filipinos "identity at a time when the Filipinos in America were non-entities, regarded only as cheap laborers."[2] Though Esperanza applied for and received a license to preach from the FAFB, later he decided to give up that license and join the AG instead.

Having decided to join the AG, Esperanza made preparations to pursue his goal of starting an AG work in the Philippines. Even while still studying at Northwest Bible Institute (NBI), he contacted Filipino Pentecostals already ministering in the Philippines, including Pedro Collado, Pedro Castro, Benito Acena, and Emil Bernaldez. Although he gained little information from these communications, he correctly ascertained that these ministers were working independently of each other. After graduating from NBI, he attended the convention of the Northwest District Council of the USAG, where he applied for and was granted a license to preach.

Esperanza then proceeded to California to inform the Filipino Pentecostal ministers there of his plan to go back to the Philippines to start an Assemblies of God mission. However, he found out that many of them had already joined the Foursquare Church, the Church of God, or the Filipino Assemblies of the First-Born. Yet there were others who were not committed to any of the existing denominations. Some were even leaning towards the Assemblies of God. Together with Esteban Lagmay, another Filipino AG minister, Esperanza planned a convention to organize an Assemblies of God group among the Filipino pastors without denominational commitments in the US. In early December 1938, the convention was held at the Upper Room Mission in San Jose, CA. Lagmay was elected President.

When Esperanza arrived in the Philippines, he personally visited pastors within the northern Luzon area, where he resided, to invite them to the organizational convention.[3] On January 20, 1940, Esperanza, Alcantara, and Abrenica met with Leland Johnson in Parañaque, Rizal to plan the convention. Johnson had arrived with his family the previous December.[4] In another meeting in Villasis, Pangasinan, on February 10, 1940, the following were appointed to serve on the convention committee: H. Abrenica, L. Sebastian, S. Obaldo, and R. Esperanza.[5] In accordance with American colonial law, Johnson would head the new organization.

In the actual convention, neither Esperanza nor the other committee members were prominent in the program. Apparently in an effort to foster unity, preaching, devotional, and worship leading assignments were given to various pastors and missionaries in attendance. Esperanza himself spoke only once, in the evening service on the day he was ordained and then elected the Secretary of what was originally called the Philippines District Council of the Assemblies of God. The PDCAG was formed under the umbrella of the USAG's Foreign Missions Department. The minutes state that the election had been a strenuous activity and people welcomed the spiritual atmosphere of the evening service.[6] No explanation is given in the minutes as to why the election was "strenuous." However, this gives the impression that the process of choosing the leaders proved to be difficult. Similar tension would surface in succeeding elections.

Promoter of the District

Esperanza's efforts to promote the PDCAG and encourage people to join the organization did not stop after the group was organized. During the Ministers' Institute sponsored by the District in 1950, he led discussions of benefits churches were to receive for affiliating with the District Council. Among many other benefits, he pointed out, "This will safeguard us from possible working advantage of the enemy to divide God's people. In the years of our church infancy we were loosely bound together but I believe that as we are growing in age and number, it seems necessary to have a more binding relationship."[7] Promotion efforts seem to have proven effective, since in those early days the District Council grew not only by the addition of individuals to AG churches but also by the affiliation of whole congregations with the fellowship. There were also instances when independent pastors resigning from their pastorates turned over their churches to District officials. For example, in northern Luzon, two congregations with doctrinal stances similar to that of the AG—a church in San Blas, Villasis, Pangasinan, and another church in Barabar, San Nicolas, Ilocos Norte—were turned over to the District Council and became members of the PDCAG.[8]

Evangelical Leader

Esperanza's diary while studying at NBI and his reports as a District and General Superintendent show that long before ecumenism was well-accepted, he was already an ecumenist. As a student at NBI, he attended several services with Presbyterians and Baptists.[9] When he returned to the Philippines, he often attended the worship services of other Pentecostal groups. Perhaps the fact that his spiritual journey led him from one religious group to another gave him his ecumenical outlook. He was born a Roman Catholic, joined the Methodists when he was in high school, was converted to Pentecostalism in the US, received a license to preach with the First-Born, and then finally joined the AG. This openness to fellowshipping with other religious groups was important as he led the PGCAG in overcoming denominational prejudices and cooperating with other Christian groups in the Philippines.

Among Pentecostal Groups

Before Esperanza returned to the Philippines, he already knew which Pentecostal groups were ministering in the country. He sought out these groups when he arrived. Although records are not clear (more on this later), it can be deduced that he represented the PDCAG when the United Pentecostal Fellowship (UPF) was organized in 1949. Organizing members were the Assemblies of God, the Filipino Assemblies of the First-Born, the New Testament Church of God, the Foursquare Church, and the United Free Gospel and Missionary Society.[10]

Esperanza's reports show that the UPF was active in holding fellowships in various member churches in northern Luzon, where the group had been organized. Towards the end of 1949, he met with "Christians of other Pentecostal groups" in the Ilocos region.[11] Then early in 1950, he attended a gathering at the United Free Gospel church, in San Nicolas. He reported that there was a fair representation of Pentecostal groups and ministers from Ilocos Norte. He noted and appreciated the oneness of spirit of their worship. "Help pray that this spirit of fellowship in worship will continue on among God's people during these closing days of time when Satan is trying to destroy God's plans by dissensions. Let us pray for a real Pentecostal Fellowship among the Pentecostal groups in the Philippines," he urged.[12]

Pastors of the other Pentecostal groups also attended AG gatherings. In the April 1951 District Council Convention, Esperanza announced, "Many of the ministers of the other member groups are here with us at this convention. Let us pray that the spirit of love and unity among all the Pentecostal groups in the Philippines will exemplify and demonstrate the desire of our Lord to have all His disciples be one."[13] Clearly, Esperanza's efforts for unity went beyond the confines of the Assemblies of God.

The following year, the UPF met in Hones, Isabela. There seems to have been a growing fear of possible proselytizing. Esperanza allayed that fear:

> There is a sweet spirit of love and wonderful fellowship and understanding existing among the member groups of…this body of Pentecostal people. We feel this is the will of the Lord that we all shall have the unity of the Spirit and the bond of peace and still be faithful to our respective Assemblies and leave inviolate our own existing member organizations.[14]

The cooperation between member groups was such that, at one point, the AG even released the District Secretary, Rosendo Alcantara, to head the Bible school of the Filipino Assemblies of the First-Born. According to Alcantara, there was a couple in the Filipino Assemblies of the First-Born that had to leave because the wife became ill. The woman prayed and the Lord told her to ask Alcantara to take the couple's place as a missionary. Even though Alcantara was re-elected as secretary, he did not accept the position because he had been invited to be the principal of the Bible school in Sta. Catalina. A word given in tongues confirmed that Alcantara was to take over the administration of that school, and the Assemblies of God released Alcantara from his post. He stayed at the Bible school for five years.[15]

The fact that Esperanza and the PDCAG in general were willing to let go of their newly re-elected District Secretary in obedience to what, to them, was the direct leading of the Holy Spirit, speaks of their desire to obey the Lord and to build the kingdom of God rather than the kingdom of the AG.

There is some confusion in the dates given by Esperanza for the organization of the UPF. In his article published in the *Pentecostal Voice*'s July 1969 issue, he stated that the UPF was organized in 1946.[16] However, in an article published in the *Bulletin*'s October 1950 issue, he gave a short historical account of how the fellowship was formed. The article states that in April 1949, invitations were sent out to other Pentecostal groups and the first exploratory meeting was held at Sta. Maria, Ilocos Sur. By June, a second meeting was held in Laoag, Ilocos Norte. In a third meeting, held in Villasis, Pangasinan, on September 27 and 28, a constitution and by-laws were presented and adopted by the five member bodies represented: the Filipino Assemblies of the First-Born, the Foursquare Churches, Grace and Glory, the Assemblies of God, and an independent church. Note, however, that the name of the newly organized group was given as the

Pentecostal Fellowship of the Philippines (PFP). It is possible that the PFP was actually a group different from the UPF. However, his April 1951 report quoted above states that it was the UPF that was organized, *"leaving inviolate our existing member organization."* The expressed purpose of the PFP was similar:

> to give expression to the inherent principles of spiritual unity and fellowship of Pentecostal believers, *leaving inviolate the existing forms of church government* adopted by its members; and recognizing that every freedom and privilege enjoyed by any church or group of churches shall remain their undisturbed possession.[17]

Moreover, Esperanza did not give further reports of meetings of the PFP while he mentioned several other UPF meetings. Thus, it is more likely that the year 1946 given in the *Pentecostal Voice* article is a typographical error, that the UPF was organized in September 1949, and that UPF, not PFP, was the official name of the group.

Among Other Evangelical Groups

The AG was welcomed with open arms by other Pentecostal groups in the Philippines, but not necessarily so by other religious sectors, including the evangelical community. As previously stated, Filipinos were mainly Roman Catholic while the evangelical community had agreed on a Comity arrangement assigning specific geographical areas of ministry for member denominations, of which the AG was not one. Not only was the AG an unwanted newcomer, it was also socially ostracized because it was considered a cult. It did not help that the early AG churches were "rural based," located away from the centers of population, with most of the workers non-high school graduates who felt intimidated by professionals. At a time when the country had a low average educational level, especially in rural areas, most AG members were ordinary farmers.[18] This is understandable and even expected in light of the fact that ordinary, uneducated, rural folks who felt oppressed by the demands of their previous religion and lacked both medical knowledge and access to medical help, would be especially attracted to the Pentecostal message of Christ as Savior and Healer.

Not only were AG members considered cultic, some non-Pentecostals even considered the AG lunatic or demonic because its members spoke in tongues.[19] Angela Salazar (now Angela Aragona) was converted in Antique in 1952. She recalls that the community's impression of the AG church was that the members were noisy and spoke strange words. The neighbors also thought that the people inside the church were crazy. The church was made of *nipa* (a kind of palm leaf), so people could see inside when the Pentecostal believers were filled with the Spirit and worshipped the Lord with uplifted hands, sometimes facing the wall. To those standing outside, it looked like they were climbing the walls.[20]

However, in areas where there were close-knit relationships, such as in Bussot, Gregorio del Pilar, a Kankanaey community in Ilocos Sur, Protestant groups cooperated with one another in Easter, Christmas, and social gatherings. Especially in Del Pilar, *bayanihan* was practiced regardless of denomination, since the whole community had the same tribal culture.[21] Marcelo Arangote, a pioneering AG pastor, says that in Aklan, initially Methodists, Baptists, and other groups avoided him. However, when they realized that Arangote was not preaching religion but salvation, they became friendly.[22] Mamerto Garsulao explains that in Villar, Antique, the Pentecostals, Seventh-day Adventists,

Baptists, and other religious groups were growing fast because people were open. Fed up with the repressive Roman Catholic Church, which had controlled them for hundreds of years, plus the sufferings they had endured during World War II, the people were willing to accept new religious teachings which gave them hope.[23]

The situation was different in Manila, however. Based on the Comity agreement, Manila was supposed to be an open city, where all denominations were free to establish churches. Esperanza reported that when finally the older denominations invited the AG to join the Comity agreement, they proposed that the AG would be given some remote places in the archipelago as their area of ministry. The PGCAG declined the invitation, explaining that "it was God's mandate for us to preach the full gospel to the whole territory of the Philippines. We have to maintain also our distinctive testimony."[24] It can be presumed that this response was not appreciated by the older evangelical denominations.

Relations with the evangelical community worsened when, in 1953, Bethel Temple was opened close to Central Methodist Church, Cosmopolitan Church, and Ellinwood Church in Manila. These churches felt threatened by the huge Assembly of God building. They were fearful that Bethel Temple would siphon members from the other Protestant churches[25]

The fear was not unfounded, because Bethel Temple's pastor, Lester Sumrall, invited several famous healing evangelists to conduct salvation and healing crusades in Manila, resulting in thousands of converts to Pentecostalism.[26] The Methodists were greatly affected when Ruben Candelaria, Superintendent of the Manila District of the Methodist Church in the Philippines, and his cousin, David Candelaria, pastor of Taytay Methodist Church, both received the Pentecostal experience of baptism in the Holy Spirit and spoke in tongues. Ruben became an AG pastor while David's church was split, with one group under David holding to their Pentecostal experience.

The evangelical community had another reason to feel threatened. In 1953, before the series of salvation and healing crusades, the AG had already gained prominence in the city and favor with the mayor when Sumrall succeeded in delivering Clarita Villanueva, a prison inmate, from demon-possession. This event received front page coverage in the country's major daily newspapers. In appreciation for Sumrall's ministry, the mayor had the building permit for Bethel Temple quickly released free of charge. Later, the mayor granted the AG use of the prominent Roxas Park for the 1954 Clifton Erickson crusade. The permit was for one month, again free of charge.[27]

This prominence and favor changed the self-image of the PGCAG members. Carmelita Gallardo observes that by the 1960s, the AG people she worked with were proud separatists. They did not join the activities of the evangelical community in Manila. Perceiving themselves to be self-sufficient, especially with the financial support of the American missionaries, their general attitude was that they could stand alone. Furthermore, the Holiness practices of the denomination led some AG members to believe that the other non-Pentecostal, non-Holiness groups were not real Christians.[28] Reflecting their Pentecostal heritage, these believers were rejected for much the same reason the US Pentecostal pioneers had been rejected. They not only displayed too much emotion and lacked social respectability, but also their perceived divisive attitudes caused ill feelings because they looked down on non-Pentecostals' spirituality.

Esperanza had to counter this separatist attitude of some sectors of the PGCAG. In the 1960s, he initiated moves for the PGCAG to join the National Council of Churches in the

Philippines.[29] He led the PGCAG in cooperating with some evangelical efforts such as the 1956 Billy Graham crusade and the Bob Pierce National Ministers Conference. However, in his article published in July 1969, Esperanza deplored the fact that as an organization, the PGCAG was aloof towards the Ecumenical Movement, and AG ministers did not want the PGCAG to seek membership in the said movement.[30] Esperanza was not able to see the fruit of his labors to build a bridge between the PGCAG and the evangelical community. It took several years more for his efforts to come to fruition.[31]

Chapter 6

Executive officers of the Philippines General Council
Pedro Castro, *Treasurer*
Rudy Esperanza, *Superintendent*
Rosendro Alcantara, *Secretary*
Source: Philippines, *Foreign Missions Department, Assemblies of God*, (1959?)

DISTRICT SECRETARY AND GENERAL SUPERINTENDENT

In the absence of a duly appointed Superintendent after the war, Esperanza requested the mother organization in the US to grant him a temporary appointment to the position so that the PDCAG could continue with its mission.[1]

The 1946 file in the PGCAG archives includes letters, certifications, and affidavits all attesting to the fact that he was both Acting Superintendent and Secretary of the PDCAG, based on the official appointment given by the USAG Missions Committee, an appointment which was likewise based on the endorsement that he had received from his fellow Filipino ministers.[2]

Noticeable in Esperanza's 1946 certification was the attached list of 18 places with AG churches having a total of more than 500 active members.[3] In comparison, in 1941, Leland Johnson had written, "From the latter part of 1939 to the fall of 1941, our five churches had multiplied to thirty four. Taking into consideration the opposition we faced, the growth truly seems phenomenal."[4] These numbers show the debilitating effect on the denomination of more than three years of war. Despite the efforts of pastors to preserve their flocks, several churches and many church members were lost during the Japanese occupation.

On April 13, 1949, during the Seventh Annual Meeting, the Filipino pastors gained greater control of the denomination when the Council in session approved a resolution eliminating the provision for the appointment of the PDCAG District Superintendent and making this an elected position. The provision for the qualifications of elected officers, including the District Superintendent, was likewise revised:

> The Officers of the District Council shall be chosen from the membership of the District Council and shall be men of mature experience and ability, who have been ordained and have been a member of the District Council for one year. A 2/3 majority [of] votes shall be necessary to constitute an election. The term of office shall begin 30 days after election.[5]

Two days later, on April 15, the Council held an election based on the approved resolutions. Esperanza was voted in as District Superintendent, thus retaining his post. Though ten missionaries were present, only one post was filled by a missionary, Clyde Shields. Shields was voted in as one of the Executive Presbyters and at the same time chosen as Presbyter of the Ilocos Sur-Abra Section. All the rest of the elected officers were Filipinos.[6]

Initial Attitude of the PDCAG Ministers toward the Leadership

In 1948, during the Sixth Annual District Council Convention, Edwin Brengle, principal of BBI, proposed that the management of the Bible school be turned over to Filipinos. In response, the Filipinos unanimously approved a motion that the Bible school management be under the American missionaries "with the cooperation of the Filipino Brethren."[7] Clearly, the Filipinos did not have the resources to run the school, which at that point was greatly dependent on USAG funding for its infrastructure and operating expenses. Thus, the Filipinos settled for "cooperation" as the extent of their participation in the running of the Bible school.

Two other motions were presented related to the work of the District Superintendent. The first motion proposed that the District Superintendent be released from his pastoral and Bible school duties so that he could devote his full time to the District. Another motion proposed that, since the District Superintendent was free to visit the churches, he could do evangelistic work so that the District would be relieved of the expense of supporting a District evangelist. Both motions were carried.[8]

The bylaws provided that the salary of the District Superintendent would be "P100.00 a month, minus his regular designated allowance, plus his traveling expenses."[9] Yet the following year, after the resolutions for the District Superintendent's election had been carried, when a resolution was put forward for the District Secretary and District Treasurer to be given a monthly allowance plus office expenses in view of the fact that their duties incurred expenses and time, the resolution was not carried.[10]

The above motions and resolutions show that the Filipino pastors were not yet ready to bear the responsibility of financially supporting their own denominational leaders. Perhaps the fact that most of the elected leaders were Filipinos who had ministered in the US before coming back to the Philippines was a factor in this reluctance. It was common knowledge that these pastors were receiving personal financial support from backers in the US. Local Filipino pastors often expected these returning pastors to share the blessings with the "less fortunate" ministers. It is likely that local Filipino pastors believed that, instead of needing financial help from the District, the District officials were duty-bound to raise funds for the organization. Indeed, Esperanza's diaries record many fund-raising preaching trips to the US.

Esperanza's Travelogue

Esperanza had a regular column called "The Superintendent's Report" in the *Bulletin*, the PDCAG's official monthly magazine. Often his reports noted which churches he had visited during the previous months. A common element in these reports was description of his long and difficult travel as he endeavored to visit as many churches scattered all over the archipelago as time and finances would allow. Frequently, however, the grueling journey was rewarded by the warm fellowship of the brethren, who were thirsty for God's word.

In July 1949 he visited the Visayas islands. He wrote:

> Sailing down from Manila to New Washington, Panay, in the General Roxas [ship] we were so crowded. We had to sleep on the deck. It was raining when we sailed. At midnight we suddenly sailed into heavy rain. When I was awaken [sic] I was already soaked to the skin. There was no canvass over our deck to protect us from the rain. The next day I had a high fever. I prayed to God to heal me before landing. In His grace He did and thank God for His power to heal.[11]

In another report, he described a challenging trip to visit the churches pioneered by Pastor Patayan and Pastor Collado in Cotabato, Mindanao. Esperanza and his party first visited the

Belaans, a tribe living in the foothills of Mt. Matutum. They passed through thick bushes and dense forests. They also walked through a jungle where "the moisture never falls" because of high humidity. Finally, to reach the Belaan village, the party had to climb a hill. After visiting this village, the group continued their trek from church to church, hiking that whole day and covering several kilometres over difficult terrain.[12]

To visit a church in Muñoz, Isabela, in northern Luzon, Esperanza rode an amphibian jeep across the swift and turbulent waters of the Magat River. He then tried to proceed to Muñoz by bus, but the buses could not cross the river. Thus, his party took off their shoes, rolled up their pants, and waded through mud. They then crossed the river in a small boat called a *banca*. To their great disappointment, the Muñoz church members were away planting rice. Esperanza and his colleagues decided to return at a more opportune time.[13]

One time, he and Pastor Obaldo visited churches in Ilocos Sur and Norte. At one point, they went to Langcuas, leaving Santa Maria by sunrise. They walked barefoot along the riverbed, walking over sharp stones and mossy rocks. Soon the hot sun was beating down upon their heads. Esperanza slipped three times before they finally reached Langcuas at 3 p.m. But when they got to the place, Esperanza exclaimed, "O! It was so wonderful to hear the mountain folks sing. Our fatigue melted away as we felt God's blessing upon us. Soon we were also singing with them." After the afternoon service in Langcuas, Esperanza and Obaldo walked another hour, reaching Cabaroan in time for the evening service. They had time for supper, and then the service began. Esperanza and Obaldo preached for an hour each, but the people wanted them to preach till daybreak. "Oh, they were so hungry of the Word," Esperanza exclaimed. The next day, the two moved on to other churches for more services.[14]

Anacleto Lobarbio was a student at BBI in the 1960s, when the PGCAG had grown to eight districts.[15] He witnessed Esperanza's dedication in travelling around the country, visiting the churches of those eight districts. On top of this, Esperanza headed the General Council convention, maintained communication with AG missionaries going in and out of the country, responded to many invitations to speak or grace affairs, and travelled abroad as part of his portfolio as General Superintendent. Amidst all these activities, Esperanza did not give up teaching at BBI and administering the school's affairs.[16]

Lobarbio developed a greater admiration for Esperanza when later he himself was elected Superintendent of the Southern Tagalog District, a position he held for twenty-four years.[17] He recalls the sacrifice that he and his family had to make for the sake of the ministry under the PGCAG. There were many instances when he left his family for extended times as he went around his district visiting pastors and their churches. Yet he had only one district; Esperanza had eight, and these were scattered all over the country. Moreover, Esperanza did not have the technology and rapid means of communication and travel available to leaders today.[18] Thus, he admired Esperanza's patience and perseverance in visiting AG churches across the country.[19]

Despite the fact that he had been used to physical labor in the US, Esperanza's more than ten years there most probably would have made him accustomed to more convenience in life. Yet not once in his many reports did he complain about his grueling trips. What could have been the motivating force that kept him going despite the difficulties of his travels among the various churches of the AG in the Philippines? A closer look at his life and his writings may give insight into his driving motivation.

Various Roles as Secretary/Superintendent

When Esperanza was elected to the position as Secretary, and later General Superintendent, of the Assemblies of God in the Philippines, he took on various roles much-needed by the young and growing denomination. Three of those roles will be dealt with in this book: as an evangelist, a mentor, and a visionary leader. This chapter will deal with the first two, leaving the last and more far-reaching role to a later chapter. It will be seen that Esperanza took on roles that already characterized him as a person long before he assumed his elected position.

Evangelist

"Spreading the gospel and winning the lost" was an ever-present ingredient in Esperanza's endeavors. First and foremost, he was an evangelist. From the time he was converted in the US, evangelism was part of his life.

It has been stated that as a young man, Esperanza was already involved in Bible studies in the Methodist church, but when he was converted he testified, "God gave me a love and burden for my people. As they moved up and down the Chinatown of Seattle, I could see them as sheep without a shepherd. I...just wept and wept for their souls."[20]

With the help of Pauline Peterson and some friends, Esperanza's first evangelistic endeavor was to start a Mission Hall for Filipinos at 610 King Street, Chinatown, Seattle. At the same time, he opened a home for Filipino Christians at 1216 Weller Street, where he himself resided. Moreover, recognizing his call to fulltime ministry, he gave up his ambition of gaining an addendum to his name or hanging a shingle outside his window, and instead enrolled in Northwest Bible Institute.[21] His regular routine while pursuing his Bible school degree was to have his devotions early in the morning, go to Northwest for his classes, return to Weller Street in the afternoon or go to the library to study, then go to the Mission Hall in the evening for services, street ministry, prayer meeting, or whatever ministry opportunity would present itself. He would often go to bed close to midnight. Even when he held summer jobs to fund his schooling, he still involved himself in ministry.[22]

Esperanza returned to the Philippines with the explicit purpose of sharing the Pentecostal gospel with his people. He often testified that the Holy Spirit had instructed him to return to his country and obey Christ's words in Mark 5:19b, "Go home to your friends, and tell them what great things the Lord has done for you, and how He has had compassion on you."[23]

When he arrived home in 1939, his family members gathered around him expecting to receive some US souvenirs or US dollars. Instead, Esperanza told them that he had brought home nothing but his Bible and a saxophone.[24] The next day, his first public activity back in his hometown was to testify at a wedding. In introducing his newfound faith, he told the people gathered, "The old 'darling' [his pet name] is dead, and now this is the new 'darling'."[25] That Sunday he gathered the children in the neighborhood for his first service. The next weekend, he went around the community and invited neighbors to a service in his home the following Sunday. Soon he had Bible studies and services in other places as well.[26]

This evangelistic zeal stayed with him through the years that he served as Superintendent of the PGCAG. He visited many churches and took every opportunity to preach wherever he went. On his second visit to Mindanao, he was on a boat full of settlers, who were bringing food and livestock, which they would use to start their new home in Mindanao. He lost no opportunity in preaching to the passengers.[27]

Esperanza gave great emphasis to the PGCAG's evangelism program. For him, every member was a witness and an evangelist. He saw evangelism as vital in the various ministries and activities of the AG churches, whether citywide crusades, open-air mass evangelism, house-to-house barrio evangelism, deaf ministry, student-center ministry, Bible student ministry, literature programs, or radio programs.[28] He fully supported the series of evangelistic and healing crusades sponsored by Sumrall in Manila in the 1950s and 1960s. He brought BBI students to the crusades to serve as counselors. He also encouraged AG churches to come with their sick and witness the power of Christ the Healer. If they could not come, he asked them to pray fervently for the crusades.[29] Esperanza also accompanied evangelists to other places in the Philippines so that the revival sparked in Manila could touch other cities wherever the evangelists went.[30]

Indeed, reaching the whole archipelago with the gospel was Esperanza's passion.[31] He intended for the Assemblies of God to cover the whole Philippines.[32] He firmly believed that a person empowered by the Holy Spirit could not desist from going forth to preach and teach the Good News.[33] His *Bulletin* reports were full of encouragement for AG constituents to preach the gospel to the whole Philippines. In one issue, he included this fervent appeal:

> As we see the map of the Philippines with its growing towns, villages, cities, and settlements without a full gospel message, we could not but see our slowness of heart to obey and fulfill the command of our Lord: "Go ye into all the world and preach the gospel." As I travel up and down the "Pearl of the Orient Seas" and see the hunger of our own people for God expressed in the request to send gospel workers, I come to realize more than ever our tremendous responsibility in fulfilling His

great commission. In the face of this task, my prayer is that may there be no seeking of self-interest or ambition but each one seek only to promote the interest of His kingdom for His honor and glory.[34]

Thus, he urged the people to seek God's leading for their specific place and task in His kingdom and then to faithfully unite efforts to win the Philippines for the Lord Jesus Christ.[35]

The underlying motive for Esperanza's evangelistic zeal was the Pentecostal theological paradigm, "Jesus is coming soon!" The majority of his "Superintendent's Reports" greeted the readers in the name of the "soon coming King." Oftentimes, he ended his reports by emphasizing the urgency of evangelism in the light of the impending end of the spiritual harvest time. Excerpts below, from closing paragraphs of his "Superintendent's Reports," reveal this sense of urgency for evangelism.

> There seems to be a spiritual recession among us. Let us seek the Lord more in praying and even fasting as the evil forces are on the increase. There is a need of power against the enemy so let us ask God to arm us with the weapons of our warfare[,] which are mighty through God to pull down the stronghold of the enemy. Let us bind ourselves together for His common interest upholding one another before the throne of grace in earnest intercession in the Holy Spirit. Dear ones, the battle is the Lord's.[36]

> Let us crown the passing year in a grand fellowship meeting where the Holy Ghost will take control at the Ministers Institute....Until then, may the Lord give you many more precious souls to be your crown of rejoicing at His coming.[37]

The urgency of the hour necessitates the pooling of our efforts and resources together in unselfish service, devotion and love to the Master. Let us work with all we have, careful of consciences and careless of our lives, and be conquerors for Jesus, showing forth indeed that we have been born from above, citizens of another world. Let us work while it is day; the night is coming when no man can work.[38]

Remember, we are passing this way, this year, just once. If we fail to live for God in this time of Harvest, great will be our failure and loss. When we finish our life's journey we are not permitted to mend our mistakes and crooked ways. This is God's year. This year is our Year. Let us spend it for God![39]

Esperanza's last message was preached on October 26, 1969, at his home church in Pozorrubio, the church he had pioneered there when he came back to the Philippines in 1939. His wife, Leonor, wrote an account of that last message:

"I was up early this morning at 3:30 and went downstairs. The sweet presence of God came mightily upon me. How strong!" These were his first words as he stood up to preach. It was a stirring message on faith, exhorting us to be faithful unto the end, emphasizing on the ingredients of faith—patience and long-suffering. "I have preached to you long ago, 30 years ago, that Jesus is coming soon. Be patient for his coming is very soon," he added. Little did we know that it was to be his last message and his last time to be with us."[40]

After Esperanza died, his congregation recalled that his last message was the same as the first message he had preached to them: that Jesus was coming again and they needed to repent.[41]

For Esperanza, the harvest was great and urgent, but the laborers were few. Something must be done to get the harvest in before it was too late. His next focus was to train laborers.

Mentor

Many people testify that Esperanza was a "people person." He mingled with people regardless of their age. In conventions he would join pastors and their wives during break time and chat with them. In gatherings he would sit and converse with the elderly. At home he would entertain his children's friends and share jokes with them.[42] Javier, one of his students at BBI, recalls him to be, most of all, a loving person.[43]

This natural love for people was crucial to Esperanza's role as head of the PGCAG because he was seen as a mentor. Esperanza's students, co-ministers, and family note that he intentionally sought to mentor them. "The growth of the denomination or the movement is also dependent upon workers trained. The future of the movement has a lot to do with the training of workers."[44] This is how Javier, PGCAG General Superintendent for almost two decades, assesses the importance of trained workers to the growth of the Assemblies of God work in the Philippines. He sees these two aspects as "twins," working "side by side." For him, this was the reason why Esperanza, despite a busy schedule, continued to be actively involved in the training of workers by teaching in Bible schools and church-based Bible training institutes.[45] As General Superintendent, Esperanza knew that the PGCAG did not have a supply of pastors commensurate to the needs of the expanding work. Sadly, the denomination had lost some churches because there were no pastors to take over when the pioneers moved.[46] Therefore, there was a strong need for more trained workers.

Being a "people person," Esperanza's method of training Bible school students both inside the classroom and outside on the field was not only through lectures but also through the personal sharing of his own life.[47] In this way, he left indelible imprints in the lives and ministries of his students.

Teacher. Many students remember Esperanza's teaching of Bible and theology subjects as "excellent." He always came prepared for his classes. They were also impressed by his good command of English albeit with an Ilocano accent.[48] His proficiency in the English language was most probably due to the fact that, aside from learning under the American school system when the Philippines was still an American colony, he had also lived in the USA for more than a decade.[49] Students also remember Esperanza's sensitivity and obedience to the move of the Holy Spirit during chapel services and classroom sessions that ended up becoming extended worship services or prayer meetings.[50] Books and lecture texts were set aside as students and faculty together spent hours in intercession and/or praise. Javier recalls:

> It was later when I was in my senior year. The subject was Hebrews and, well, as you might know, Hebrews is a very interesting book, to say the least. And many times in the class, the Holy Spirit will move and he would allow the movement of the Holy Spirit. Set aside the lesson for the day and just let the Holy Spirit touch the hearts of the students. And so the class will be turned into prayer and praise, and the Spirit will move, many will be filled with the Spirit in the classroom. That's how he conducted his classes, very open to the Holy Spirit.[51]

Esperanza taught not only in classrooms. His words expressed in other situations spoke volumes to his students. One day, some enthusiastic BBI male students asked him to donate a

PA system which they would use "to turn the world upside down for Jesus." The gist of Esperanza's response was:

> You do not, as yet, seem to understand clearly the manner how God operates His work. His ministers go proclaim His Word in the demonstration of the Spirit's power with signs following. And through God's saving power, man could receive salvation for his soul by grace through faith…without assistance from a PA system.[52]

To the graduating students of Class 1969 of Luzon Bible Institute, he wrote:

> Preachers are not sermon-makers, but men-makers and saint-makers. Although you will soon be out of the wall of your Alma Mater, continue to have Him make you a saint. God is not much concerned in great learning or great [p]reachers as much as men and women great in faith, great in holiness and great in love and compassion for lost and fallen humanity.[53]

Many of his students later became teachers in Bible schools. For example, among those interviewed for this paper, Javier, Lobarbio, and Lazaro all became faculty members of at least one AG Bible school. His principles and values modeled before them were his teaching legacy. Yet what his former students remember most were the times he fellowshipped with them outside the classroom.

Bible School Administrator.[54] When Esperanza served as BBI President and later as Dean, he often dropped in on students during their study times. He would go around and check on the men in their dorms even after dark. He would chat with the students, asking them about their studies, their experiences, their problems.⁵⁵ Those were the times when he impacted their lives the most. Students were amazed that the General Superintendent of the denomination would come down to their level and take time to talk to them, mere teenagers. They saw that he was not only friendly, but he was also humble.⁵⁶ Indeed, his humility and meekness impressed many.⁵⁷

The BBI male dorm students were assigned to guard the campus at night in two-hour shifts. As Dean, Esperanza personally took it upon himself to wake up the guards when it was time for their duty. During the day, sponsored students had to work from 2-5 p.m., while paying students were to spend the afternoon studying. Again, Esperanza would wake up the students from their afternoon siesta and call them to either work or study, as the case may be. This practice became a pattern that subsequent deans followed.⁵⁸

The Esperanzas lived in one of the houses on the BBI campus when both Rudy and Leonor were teaching in the Bible school. There were many times when Esperanza would buy *boling*, a kind of bun sold in Malinta in those days. He would then call students over to the house during the morning break for some coffee. Doubtless there were many heart-to-heart talks and bonding times over a cup of coffee and some *boling*.⁵⁹

Esperanza really cared for the youth. He was known as a "friend of the young."⁶⁰ Sometimes during summer and Christmas breaks some foreign students or students from Mindanao would not be able to go home. Esperanza "adopted" these students during the break and brought them to his home in Pozorrubio. He even took in young people to stay with his family and sent these young people to school.⁶¹ He saw potential in young people who he knew would be powerful tools in the Lord's work. He saw the youth as "future leaders of the Assemblies of God."⁶² Thus, he challenged young people to go to Bible school to prepare for ministry, and he personally helped them when they responded to the call for full-time service.[63]

One typical example was Deborah (Onggao) Lazaro, who had first met Esperanza in 1962 when the latter came to Iloilo City to meet with AG pastors in the area. She was struck by the General Superintendent's conservatism yet warm friendliness. What stunned her was when, "out of the blue," Esperanza encouraged her to pursue God's calling. That was the confirmation she needed to follow the Lord in full-time ministry. The following school year, Lazaro decided to go to BBI without any assurance of financial support. To her great surprise, Esperanza, with Pastor Lorenzo Panaguiton, met her at the Port of Manila. It was "a humbling honor" for Lazaro to be picked up by no less than the president of BBI.[64]

More surprises awaited her at BBI. Esperanza must have seen her giftings, and he provided her with opportunities to develop her potential. Lazaro describes one of those opportunities:

> I was enrolled at the Bible School with high recommendations from him [Esperanza]. He was a God-sent man. [He paved] the way for a rewarding and fulfilling ministry life for me. He believed I [could] be something for Jesus. As a freshman student, through his recommendations again, [I] was entrusted with certain responsibilities only fit for higher level students, but the man of God believed...I [could] do it...and so did I by God's grace, in all spirit of respect to the man of God, and humility of heart before the Lord I serve! As freshman, with his approval as school president, [I] was chosen to direct the 100-voice BBI choir [in singing the "Hallelujah" chorus of Handel's "Messiah"] during the 1963 BBI Graduation Exercises at Manila Bethel Temple. Together with my Music Instructor, Louise Horst, the

man of God believed I could do it, when I was scared to death to do it. My first attempt, O, my! And it was hard work I had to learn to do, but [I] was able to do it because the president said, "You can do it, Debbie."⁶⁵

From Esperanza, Lazaro learned "to live by faith, and to believe Him to see greater things in [her] obedience." She concluded, "As leader of a growing denomination, he was out enriching lives whose potential he perceived could continually be nourished and enhanced." "Rudy Esperanza was an incredible mentor by principle and by his inspiring attitude and authentic example."⁶⁶ Lazaro was one of the many AG pastors ushered into the ministry through the influence of Esperanza. She now heads her own ministry group in the US and regularly visits the Philippines to minister to local pastors and their churches.

Esperanza's mentoring did not cease after the students graduated from BBI. He visited them in their pastorates even in far-flung places. He encouraged those having difficulties in the ministry. He extended financial blessings. He often travelled with pioneer pastors, visiting their outstations no matter how difficult the trek was. If possible, he brought along another district official, and when it was time to preach or teach, the blessed opportunity to minister to the people was shared with other pastors.

The ministry of female pastors and pastors' wives was accepted in Pentecostal circles even in those early days. In fact, on March 26, 1940, Lucia Ramos, a female pastor, was among the eleven pastors who were the first ministers to be given licenses to preach by the PDCAG when the denomination was organized. The following day, two more female ministers, Encarnacion Bonuan and Gemima Cayao, were given licenses as well.⁶⁷

With this background, Esperanza likewise recognized the crucial roles of women. He considered female ministers as important as male pastors. He would chat with pastors and their wives as well, cracking jokes and spending time bonding.[68] He supported women's groups and spent time praying with their leaders.[69]

Esperanza's influence was not only due to the major ministerial roles he played, but also because of his personal qualities that made him well-suited to lead his young denomination. Those personal qualities will be considered in the next chapter.

Chapter 7

The Rodrigo Esperanza family. Behind them is the Willy's jeep
students jokingly called the "tank."
Source: Esperanza Collection, APRC archives

PERSONAL LEADERSHIP QUALITIES

A leader's characteristics determine the kind of influence that leader would make on the organization and the people he or she leads and mentors. In the course of this research on the life of Rev. Rodrigo Esperanza, several of his qualities stood out, explaining why the AG constituents kept voting him to the top office of the denomination until the Lord called him home to his eternal reward.

Encourager

Esperanza's youngest son, Danny, was often told that his father was an encourager, especially among those having difficulty in the ministry. He encouraged pastors to go on, to move in the power of the Spirit. Some pastors even told Danny, "If not for your father, I would not be in the ministry right now."[1]

Darlino Gumallaoi was one pastor who was encouraged by Esperanza. Esperanza would counsel Gumallaoi as the young pastor accompanied him in his visits to churches in Pangasinan. Since the support from Gumallaoi's pioneering church was meager, Esperanza committed to send him ₱20 per month. Back then, that amount went a long way toward meeting the pastor's needs.[2]

Gumallaoi recalls Esperanza's frequent advice: "Just do the work as a pastor then the Lord will bless your work....Remain faithful to the Lord and he will be faithful to you." This advice kept Gumallaoi in the ministry for almost fifty years, trusting the Lord in the midst of difficulties and even turning down an offer of a position in the US.[3] Gumallaoi is thankful to Esperanza for believing in him and trusting that he would persevere in the ministry long after Esperanza had gone on to his eternal rest.[4]

Rebecca LagmayAlimbuyao likewise believes that Esperanza had the gift of encouraging people. She remembers many times when Esperanza would visit her father, Romulo Lagmay, a pastor, and spend time talking with him. Often he would say, "Romulo, just keep up the good work." Alimbuyao's mother was active in the Women's Ministry, and Esperanza would also spend time with her and pray with her. For Alimbuyao, no one mentored her father aside from Esperanza. Alimbuyao, who now pastors her own church, says that Esperanza's example has impacted her ministry. She is a firm believer in mentoring, "because without mentoring, these good values of our Christian experiences or Christian conduct will not be passed on to others. So mentoring is really important so that the vision, and...the things that we receive from God will continuously be carried out."[5]

Esperanza's encouragement was not limited to ministers. Esperanza was an encourager by nature. He sought to encourage everyone in his or her Christian walk. His nephew, Jesse Bautista, was a young sailor in the US Navy. Bautista would receive letters from Esperanza asking how he was doing. In each letter, his Uncle Rudy exhorted him, "Just be strong in the Word always....I know there are so many temptations, but you have to get strong every day."[6] Bautista is now retired from the US Navy. He remains true to the faith his uncle introduced to him when he was still a youth.

Man of Prayer and of the Word

Carmelita Gallardo was a new convert when she was hired to help the PGCAG headquarters as assistant recording secretary. From her Roman Catholic background, she brought with her a concept of priests and pastors as being beyond the reach of ordinary parishioners. Because of this, early on, she approached Esperanza with great trepidation. She treated him with great respect. The man was calm, quiet, and dignified. Their relationship was professional, yet he literally had an "open door policy." Whenever he was in his office, his office door would be open. Many times Gallardo reported to work and saw, through the open door, Esperanza already at his table, head bowed, arms folded, and a Bible on the table. Imagine her awe yet delight when the General Superintendent befriended her and showed her real concern, treating her not merely as a secretary but as a sister in the Lord.

Gallardo can never forget the first time Esperanza passed by her table and saw her troubled face. He stopped and gently inquired what her problem was. After she shared her problem, he said, "Let's pray." Esperanza's prayer was specific. He mentioned the names of people; he prayed for specific events and situations;

he asked for specific answers. That experience was followed by many more prayer and counseling times because he often asked about her family. He told her that if she would put God's kingdom first in her life, God would give her everything else she needed. He exhorted her to rejoice when times were abundant and also to rejoice when times were difficult. Moreover, she was to honor Jesus now on this earth so that when she went to heaven, Jesus would honor her also. Only later, when she was regularly reading her Bible, did she find out that Esperanza's counsel was actually lifted from the Scriptures. He did not quote the book, chapter, and verse, but Scripture naturally flowed out of his lips as he counseled and comforted her.

Soon, a close bond developed between the two. Esperanza was like a father to her. She became close to the Esperanza family and was treated as a member of the household.[7] Esperanza so impacted Gallardo's spiritual growth that it is no wonder Gallardo's present ministry style is patterned after that of the late General Superintendent. According to her, the way she prays, the way she preaches, and the way she handles the congregation she is pastoring now are all influenced by Esperanza.[8]

Humble

As mentioned earlier, the fact that Esperanza would descend to the level of teenage Bible school students and mingle with them was awe-inspiring to his students. He did not consider it below his status to attend to the needs of students and pastors. It was Esperanza's humility that personally impacted Javier.[9]

One outward manifestation of Esperanza's humility was his jeep. Javier explains why:

Pastor Esperanza had this all-metal jeep. I don't know where it was assembled....And we would jokingly call it a "tank," because every time he would drive into the campus after his trips probably in the provinces, we already knew that it was Pastor Esperanza because the jeep was rattling all the way from the gate to his house. So jokingly we called it a "tank." And I sort of resented that because...that was the time when every American AG missionary would drive a brand-new car when they came. Later on of course that policy was changed.[10]

Esperanza's daughter, Lydia, describes that jeep in greater detail. It was a "Willys" jeep assembled in the Philippines with a galvanized iron body.[11] When it was on the road, it was noisy because the metal vibrated. Moreover, "[W]hen it's hot, it's like an oven. When it's cold, you'll freeze in there." It was bought with Speed the Light offerings from the USAG, and Esperanza drove it as he visited the churches in Luzon.[12] He did not seem to mind that his service jeep was uncomfortable and noisy. He never argued that a man of his position deserved a much better vehicle.

In the earlier times, Esperanza's duties as District Secretary necessitated that he step into the pulpit of churches that had no pastor. He filled in as pastor of a church in Sta. Maria Norte in Binalonan, fulfilling not only the pulpit ministry, but also conducting Bible studies and visiting sick people. He reported that the condition of one cripple that he had prayed for was greatly improved. The man was able to walk a kilometer without the use of his cane. The man's remarkable healing led the wife to receive Christ as her Savior. Moreover, curious people came to church to see the man for themselves. This led to an increase in church attendance.[13]

One would have expected a busy denominational leader to refuse to be tied down to a single church. Esperanza's report does not describe how large the church congregation was nor where the church was located. Even today, Binalonan is a small town. It must not have been prosperous in 1949, when Esperanza temporarily took over the pastoral duties of the AG church in Sta. Maria Norte. However, Esperanza did not consider it beneath himself to serve as pastor of a small-town church. His love for ministering to people was such that he was willing to extend himself when the situation required it. In fact, in one report, he spent New Year's Eve away from home because he was ministering in Isabela and baptizing converts.[14]

A much more sensitive situation in the 1960s highlights the man's humility. At that time, it was considered a great honor to pastor Manila Bethel Temple, the biggest AG church in the country, situated in the heart of the Philippines' premier city. Sumrall, the church's senior pastor, chose Ruben Candelaria to be one of the pastors. Some people believed that Esperanza could have been General Superintendent and pastor Bethel Temple at the same time. Although he had only graduated from a Bible institute, while Candelaria had graduated with honors from Union Theological Seminary in Manila, some pastors considered Esperanza well-qualified and worthy of the honor of pastoring Manila Bethel Temple. However, pastors did not sense any atmosphere of competition between him and Candelaria. "And later, when Rev. Ruben Candelaria was elected as General Treasurer, [Esperanza] was happy because to him the influence on the Candelarias was a sort of a feather in his hat when these two giants of the Methodist Church became Pentecostal."[15]

Pictures in the APRC archives support the above observation. It was common practice for the head of an organization to be standing or sitting at the center of a group picture. In many group photos of Esperanza, however, other people take center stage. There is one particular picture in which the two Candelarias are in the front row center, on opposite sides of an American evangelist. Esperanza is on the right side of the second row. Photos such as this give the viewer an idea of the willingness of the General Superintendent to allow others to take the place of honor commonly given to someone of his position.

Man of Integrity

Lydia tells of pastors looking up to Esperanza because he had contributed much to build up the integrity of Christians, especially ministers.[16] It is often said that the most common causes of a pastor's downfall are the 3 G's: gold, girls, and glory. Esperanza carefully guarded his integrity against these three. A primary focus was his integrity in handling finances. As head of a denomination, he was often entrusted with money. He kept detailed accounts of his receipts and disbursements. His diaries are peppered with numbers: offerings received, prices of items bought, room rates of hotels, exact fare paid for his travels, postage paid, etc.[17] He maintained ledgers in which various monies were recorded under headings according to their designation: personal offerings, funds for special projects, funds directly given, etc. Every debit or credit was listed. Likewise, his Superintendent's Reports were transparent in regards to finances. Moreover, he willingly used his personal funds for official business travel or purchases when PGCAG funds were insufficient. Most of all, aware of the fact that the denomination had been struggling with funds from the start, in those early days he did not accept the full allowance allotted to him as General Superintendent. Instead, he helped pay for office expenses. Below is an excerpt from his report on this matter during the Fifth General Council Convention:

May I wish to state that as soon as I had assumed office in May 1961, I moved my family to Malinta, Valenzuela, Bulacan. We have moved from one house to another three times until a year ago we landed into one of the houses of Bethel Bible Institute. Our General Treasury gave us our house rent as much as it could. It was due to our strained financial condition that made me decide to accept the teaching job and the presidency of Bethel Bible Institute.

May I wish also to correct the impression of not a small number of our brethren that I am drawing from our Treasury a monthly salary of ₱300.00 as stipulated in our budget. I have been drawing a salary of ₱150.00 only. This is due to the fact that I have been receiving some offerings from churches and friends from the United States. I have been giving our tithes to the General Council Treasurer and had contributed ₱12.00 for telephone, ₱7.00 for electricity, and contributed for about a year ₱20.00 for rent.[18]

This report was made in view of the fact that a resolution had been approved in 1948 during the Sixth District Council stating that "the District Superintendent [should] be released from his pastoral and Bible school duties so that he could devote his full time to the District."[19] The report implies that there were rumors and complaints going around about the monetary remuneration Esperanza was receiving. Apparently, the complaints did not stop. Two years later, in his report at the Sixth General Council Convention, Esperanza once again detailed the allowance he was receiving from the PGCAG:

First of all, in addition to the normal functions of the office you had elected me to occupy, I had committed myself, and my wife likewise, to continue to teach in Bethel Bible Institute. This is due to just one reason: the inability of our General Council to provide a parsonage or house rent. For our teaching services we are provided a house, electricity, water, student help and cash. The aggregate amount including cash for both of us is ₱134.00. During the last two years I have been drawing from the General Council Treasury a monthly allowance of ₱100.00, and also travel expenses when necessary.

Instead of requesting an increase in allowance, or simply drawing the full P300 monthly amount, Esperanza even decreased the monthly allowance he withdrew from the Treasury from ₱150 to ₱100. He once again stressed that his teaching at BBI was to help augment his family's resources. He had four children for whom he needed to provide. Although he was receiving some support from friends he had made when he was still in the US and when he was studying at Northwest, this amount was usually shared with other ministers who needed help.[20]

Esperanza did all this because he wanted AG ministers to be consistent in word and practice. He constantly stressed that life from "inside out" was what was crucial to God. One who is holy "inside" must also be holy "outside." He reminded people that the matters of the heart should align with biblical principles. He had strong Bible-based convictions, and he sought to please the Lord and refused to compromise God's standard of truth and righteousness.[21]

Persevering

As head of a growing denomination, Esperanza not only faced myriad duties, he also faced various problems and challenges. Basically, there were two roots of the problems: lack of funds and lack of workers. Often these two roots were intertwined.

The AG work in the Philippines was beset by a lack of funds which hampered the expansion of its various ministries. The denomination's ministries were funded mainly by the ministers' and churches' tithes. This was stipulated in the PGCAG Constitution. All members pledged to obey its stipulations. However, not all were fulfilling their obligations. After WWII, the denomination resumed its annual national conventions in 1946. At the 1948 convention, the District Treasurer reported that some churches were not faithful in fulfilling their obligations to the District.[22] The denomination also decided to collect Home Missionary offerings as a source of funds for churches applying for loans. Here the Council had a two-pronged problem: giving had been low and loans that were supposed to have been fully paid within one year still had balances due.[23] Moreover, though the various districts were supposed to give one offering a year for general office expenses and two offerings a year for the support of the two Filipino teachers in the Bible school, again giving had been low.

In 1950, the General Superintendent made repeated calls urging the pastors and churches to send their financial support. In one report, he reminded the pastors that the Council had passed a resolution that the first Sundays of July and November were Bible School Sundays. Churches were supposed to take an offering for the Bible school's Filipino teachers, but not all complied. Recognizing that not all members could give cash, he made concessions. He encouraged those who did not have money instead to give "rice, vegetables, chickens, pigs, fruits, and other things to eat." These were valued according to the current prices, and credit was given to the donating churches in the Council records.[24]

The next year, Esperanza made another call for the Bible school offering to aid in the "training of our young people who will carry the message of the Full Gospel to every nook and cranny of the Philippines."[25] Still response was slow. So Esperanza dedicated his Superintendent's Report the following year to call for pastors and co-workers to take up the designated offerings for the support of the two Filipino Bible school faculty and to give half of their tithes to the District for General Office operating expenses. He reminded the pastors, "Although the paying of tithes into the District Treasury is not the basis of fellowship but that of voluntary co-operative fellowship, yet we expect each minister affiliated with the District Council to support the District Offices." He closed his report with a plea, "Your much needed cooperation and loyalty to the Fellowship is requested."[26]

For various reasons, Esperanza's call for financial support received a poor response. Many ministries of the PGCAG were seriously affected by the constant lack of funds.

In 1958, Tommy Lee Osborn, an American Pentecostal evangelist, author, and founder of T. L. Osborn Ministries, developed a program for training and supporting local pioneering pastors every month for one year, after which the church was supposed to be able to stand on its own.[27] Filipino AG pioneers were among the recipients of the monthly support. However, it was stipulated that the pioneers must submit monthly reports of their work. Moreover, at the end of one year, the pioneer must open another pioneering work. If these stipulations were not followed, the support would stop.

To keep the support coming, financially strapped pastors would stay in their pioneering work for only one year and then move on to another pioneering work, regardless of whether the previous work could stand on its own, or whether another pastor was available to take over the work they left. This led to many pioneering works being started, but not growing, and even dying.[28] Esperanza addressed this issue in his annual report at the Sixth General Council Convention. He likewise informed the pastors and church delegates of the Council's difficulty in selecting pioneers because of the new, stringent rules of the Osborn Ministries. Pioneer workers were encouraged to stick to their pioneering work because many applications for support were being turned down, even those previously approved. Esperanza encouraged the pastors, "I believe we must adopt, now and with increasing momentum the Biblical principle, the indigenous principles. We must be prepared and adjust to any eventuality."[29]

The problem of workers was not limited to the Osborn-supported pioneers. From the denomination's early years, Esperanza often reported of expansions in the PGCAG's work, but these were curtailed by the insufficient supply of pastors:

> There has been expansion in many places, new territories invaded even when handicapped by a lack of workers. There are few places which have not been making any headway at all but seem to have been undergoing times of purging. Some outstations, due to lack of workers have been neglected and have died out.
>
> The mountain works in Ilocos Sur and in Benguet are moving steadily forward. God is blessing this underprivileged people in [a] wonderful manner. The expansion of these works is being limited due to the lack of workers, as we have in any other section of our field.[31]

In other instances, the AG lacked workers because funds were insufficient to support willing ones to be trained and sent out. Oriel Dumanon, writing as one of the AG leaders, points to the intertwining of the two problems of lack of funds and lack of workers. He bewails the fact that "Filipino Christians remain beginners, if not in the nursery, of Christian stewardship. As has been said, it is often true, 'We have the mission and the men, but where's the money?'"[31]

The denomination's financial challenges necessitated appeals from the General Superintendent for more support. A *Pentecostal Voice* article on the Seventh General Council Convention presented the "grave responsibilities" facing the PGCAG constituents:

> One of these responsibilities is the problem of supporting the Church and her programs. The activities of the church have greatly expanded which need more support in finances and personnel. The body in session has discussed this problem and the Holy Spirit has helped mightily in the messages and deliberations. It has been the consensus during the convention that since the church has grown already it is time now that we support all our programs. It is for this reason that the Rev. Rudy Esperanza, incumbent and re-elected general superintendent, enjoined all ministers, pastors, Christian workers, church members as well as all districts to work harder and support the General Council of the Assemblies of God in the Philippines so that all its programs, especially its missionary program, will advance.[32]

Giving added weight to the General Superintendent's challenge was the editorial of the same *Pentecostal Voice* issue. The just-concluded General Council Convention spent long discussions on the persistent PGCAG problem of supporting the denomination. The editor published his analysis and critique of the issue, giving the reader deeper insight into the matter:

> ...Indeed for these past years the movement has been going on without definite budgets for its different departments. Even the budget for the maintenance of the General Council headquarters has not been planned and figured for a whole fiscal year. Yes, much money had passed in our accounting books. But this is not the point. The point is to have a planned, systematic budget for a complete fiscal year of operation....
>
> The activities of the different departments have been hampered by the lack of a definite budget. For how can they operate without funds for their operations. [sic] Most of the expenses have been borne out either by the officers themselves from their personal money or from subsidies outside the Philippines. We have been relying heavily from the latter.[33]

Some sectors of the AG constituents explained that the denomination's financial difficulty and reliance on foreign funding were due to the Philippines being an underdeveloped country. Moreover, the denomination was still young. The editor firmly disagreed, pointing to the *Iglesia ni Cristo*, a Filipino indigenous religious group that built chapels throughout the Philippines using money collected entirely from members. Also, the editor pointed out that the PGCAG was already 27 years old. He proceeded to give his own analysis of why the PGCAG was continually plagued by a lack of funds:

We believe that the reasons why we do not have enough funds to support our whole operation are: lack of stewardship education among our constituency, lack of systematic methods of raising funds, and, inaction by our officials in solving this vital part of our ministry....

Another reason is that we have grown tremendously and have organized ourselves in the most sophisticated way without first considering our finances and local conditions. Thus we have a perfect organization complete with different departments and officers but an immobile and inactive one. This is so, because we do not have enough funds to support it and keep it going. [And yet, statistics show] we have enough resources from which to draw a well-coordinated and systematic program of financing our work here in the Philippines.[34]

In May 1969, during the Eighth General Council Convention, Esperanza gave his last annual General Superintendent's Report. In it, he spoke of the need to die to self in order to multiply.[35] About five months after giving this report, Esperanza sealed his words with his own life. He passed away in his sleep on October 26, 1969. On the first day of the memorial services held in the BBI chapel, Alcantara, the PGCAG General Secretary, said of him, "He was able to endure suffering in Christ. Although he was sick, he kept on working for the Lord....I think he did the best of his life...He can be an example for each of us to follow."[36]

Esperanza was by no means perfect. However, time has a way of dimming the negatives and leaving mostly the positives in one's memory of a person who was highly regarded. I believe it was this high regard for their leader and teacher that led individuals touched by Esperanza's life and ministry to give the following opinions of their mentor.

For Lobarbio, Esperanza had the gift of leadership. Lobarbio acknowledges that during Esperanza's time, it was difficult to lead. He comments that it is not easy to start a work from nothing, but Esperanza did it well. Despite all the difficulties, Esperanza stayed; he persevered. From the late General Superintendent, Lobarbio learned that in the ministry one must persevere, must simply "go on – on and on and on and on."[37]

Javier, after pausing in deep thought, gave this assessment of Esperanza's leadership:

> And as I said, he is a model to us. I could not identify any weakness on his part. And I believe at that time he was really the man for the Assemblies of God; no one else. And when his time was up the Lord took him. But especially from the beginning, very beginning,...1953 when the District Council became a General Council, up to 1969, his leadership was outstanding. Yes.[38]

Lazaro likewise could not identify any weakness in Esperanza. She expressed the legacy of the late General Superintendent in a nutshell:

> The late Rev. Rodrigo C. Esperanza made his deliberate choice to preach and teach God's Word in his country, and decided not to return to the United States anymore where he could have lived his life more comfortably well. His 'once and for all' response to God's bidding to return home, and tell his friends what great things the Lord had done for him in the United States, ushered the glorious birth of a God-ordained organization which has moved on fruitfully...growing, expanding, and extending out,

and which has become the Philippines General Council of the Assemblies of God...and which to this day, still reaching out, fulfilling the mandate of the Great Commission, which was the continuing burning passion of the late Rodrigo C. Esperanza for the PGCAG to keep aflame its fire until Jesus Christ returns for His bride!

The spiritual legacy he left behind is his undying love to see more Filipinos come to know Jesus in a personal way and receive Him as Savior and Lord of life. He dreamed to see many church groups planted across the islands, Spirit-filled converts become Christ's disciples, and Bible Schools producing committed workers for the growing harvest field. [39]

Irving De Mesa, a former student now pastoring an established church in Cavite City, sums it up succinctly: "He led by example. He was Godly."[40] Esperanza's godly example was the best motivation for other pastors, especially those who had sat under his ministry, to follow his lead.

Family Man[41]

To a Filipino, no matter how successful a person is in his workplace, that success is empty if it does not impact his immediate and extended family. Rudy Esperanza was a mentor to others around him, and more so with his own children.

Rudy and Leonor had four children: Rudy Jr., Rebecca, Lydia, and Daniel ("Danny"). The family was living on the BBI campus in Malinta, Polo, Bulacan by the time Lydia was born in 1956. Residing on a Bible school campus is like living in a fish bowl. A family's life is open for all to see. It was so with the Esperanzas.

Javier was living on the campus as a dorm student in the mid-1950s. Thus, he was able to observe the Esperanza family. He recalls that Rudy was "a loving husband and a doting father to his children." He considers it unusual for an Ilocano to be a "touch person," but Rudy would always hug his kids, especially when he would return from one of his travels. The children were happy when their father came home.[42]

One of his nieces, Rebecca Alimbuyao, confirmed that Rudy was a "touch person." Rudy would visit the Lagmay family at the Bible school in Pangasinan. Rebecca recalls that when the children would come home from school, Rudy would grab them and say, "Give Uncle a hug."[43]

The Esperanzas' home was like an inn. People were in and out of the house all the time. The family frequently had visitors: pastors from the north and south of the country, missionaries and other foreigners, staff, students, etc. Many were invited for tea after chapel services or for dinner, which Leonor loved to prepare with the help of students. Should unexpected guests arrive, it was standard practice that the children would give up their places at the dining table and transfer to the kitchen, where they had another table.

The Esperanza's generosity went beyond sharing food. Rudy would give his polo shirts or even his *barong* to other pastors. At times he would give them bus or boat fare to go back home. Some who came with problems ended up staying in the house. Visiting pastors would be seen in their home at any time of the day.

This situation did not create any resentment in the family, however, because the children were brought up to honor the pastors. After the meal, the children would gather around the visitors and ask for stories. This was quite unusual; in many Filipino homes at that time, children were not allowed to join in the conversations of adults. Yet those visits were enriching times for the children as they met various kinds of people. The children would especially enjoy the visit if the visitors brought along their own children.

Living on the campus, the Esperanza family followed the campus schedule. Like the students, they had devotions at 6:30 p.m., but theirs lasted much longer, because every child had to pray. Sunday service was also a must. Rudy no longer pastored when he took over the helm of the PGCAG. Still, he saw to it that the whole family went to church together, attending both Sunday school and the worship service. When they arrived home after the service, Rudy quizzed the children, especially the older siblings: "What was the message? What was the theme? What was the text? What did you do in Sunday school? What did you learn today?"

Rudy trained his children not only in spiritual things but also in practical life. Everyone had responsibilities in the house. Just as he had been trained while growing up, his children likewise had chores to do when they came home from school in the afternoon.

One day Rudy bought a German Shepherd. The dog was not only to guard the house but also a way to teach the Esperanza children how to love animals and be responsible in caring for them. Rudy himself loved pets, so he taught his kids how and what to feed the dog, how to give the dog a bath, and how to train the dog. This love for dogs and other pets stayed with the whole family.

Rudy's love for planting was also passed on to his children. On the BBI campus, each of his children had his or her own garden plot. They planted vegetables such as *pechay*, bell peppers, and *ampalaya*. Moreover, Rudy oftentimes brought the children to their grandfather's farm in Pozorrubio so they would see how rice was planted and harvested. He believed that if his children saw how difficult it was to plant and harvest rice, they would not waste a single grain.

The family raised chickens, pigs, turkeys, and geese. They even had fish in the fishpond on the BBI campus. The children had to attend to the plants, the animals, and the fish early in the morning and in the afternoon. Later in life, the children appreciated the discipline of rising early and taking care of the plants and animals. Their father was teaching them to be self-sufficient, not to be dependent on what they could buy from the market. This lesson on self-sufficiency has been passed on to the children's children.

Alimbuyao relates a conversation with her Uncle Rudy which is now deeply embedded in her memory. It was one of those weekends when Rudy visited his home in Pozorrubio. He often invited the Lagmay kids to come over to their house to read and to spend time in his orchard picking *chico*, bananas, lemons, *calamansi*, or oranges. This time he explained to the children that when he planted anything that would bear fruit, he was not the only one benefitted. Instead, he loved to share the fruit with other people. He said, "You plant not only for yourself, but for other people." Moreover, he said, "I planted this and that's why you are here to share some of the fruits. Come here and let's enjoy [these] together." Long after this conversation, Rebecca still remembers, "[W]hen we do something, it's not only for ourselves, but also for other people."[44]

Along with all his loving ways, Esperanza was also a disciplinarian. Danny said that his father was strict. One time Danny lost his slippers. His father spanked him and told him to think hard and try to recall where he left his slippers. His father brought him to the places where he had gone that day until they finally found his slippers. Later Danny understood. His father did not look for his slippers; he had to do it himself, but his father guided him to where he had left his slippers. He appreciated his father for doing that.

Rudy believed in spanking. However, he made sure his child understood the reason for the spanking. He would ask, "Why are you being spanked? What is your offence? How many [spanks] do you want?" Each disciplinary action ended with a hug, an assurance that the erring child was still loved.

One wonders how Rudy could still spend time with his family in view of his frequent trips. Lydia explains that when her father came home in the afternoon, he would look for everybody. He would check to see that the children were doing their homework. Then there were the regular evening devotions. When he would be gone for an extended period of time, he would write to his family. He would send letters, cards, or postcards. He would have a message for each child, which Leonor would read to the child. He would remind his children to keep on serving God. Lydia treasures a postcard her father sent her when he was in the US for a considerable length of time. On that card he wrote, "Always shine for Jesus."

What he did for other young people, he also did for his children: he would tell them, "When you grow up, you will study and preach." He encouraged them to serve God and go to Bible school. Indeed, of his four children, three are now in the ministry. His daughter Rebecca studied at BBI and did her practicum in the church of Pastor De Mesa. Pastor De Mesa's comment was a tribute to Rudy: "Rebecca his daughter did her practicum in the church I was pastor. I can tell she was brought up by a great father."[45]

Although Rudy sought to make time for his children, time with his wife was often sacrificed. The philosophy of ministers during the 1950s was, "It's better to burn out than to rust out."

Missionaries and national pastors were often on the go. Emphasis was always on the ministry. There was no time for ministerial couples to go on a date away from the demands of ministry.[46] It was a great advantage that Leonor was a minister in her own right. As much as possible, Rudy and Leonor ministered together. When Rudy had invitations, he would bring his wife, and the children would stay home. When he travelled for extended periods, the couple maintained a constant flow of letters.

Danny wishes that he had known his father better. By the time he was born, the PGCAG had expanded and the demands on Esperanza were greater. When he passed away, Rudy Jr. was 19 and in his third year of college, Rebecca was 18 and in her second year of college, Lydia was 13 and in her first year of high school, while Danny was 10 and in grade four.[47] People told Danny that his father was kind and great, and that they had learned a lot from his father. Yet Danny's response was, "I have not learned so much from my father because he died early."

Lydia had more memories of her father. One of the most precious things a daughter could say of her father came from Lydia's lips. She declared, "I see him not just [as] a father, but...a spiritual leader as well....He would see to it that we go to church, that we pray, that we memorize the Word...He wanted the Word of God to be invested...in our hearts. That's the best legacy that he left us: the legacy of faith."

This lasting legacy extended far beyond his family and his organizational abilities as the top leader of the PGCAG.

Chapter 8

BBI in Pozorrubio circa 1940's. BBI was founded in Baguio but was moved to the Esperanza's property in Pozorrubio after WWII.
Source: Esperanza Collection, Asia Pacific Research Center, APTS, Baguio City

VISIONARY LEADER

Esperanza was a dreamer of big dreams for God's kingdom. This is his third and last role that will be considered in this book. Esperanza was a dreamer, but he did more than dream; he strove hard to see his dreams turned into reality. Moreover, he had the ability to look beyond current situations to future possibilities. For example, after visiting a church in Marbel, Cotabato, he reported the following assessment: "Marbel has a good size congregation with tremendous possibilities. This is the most prosperous town in Koronadal. It has two high schools and soon to have a college. It is a center of population. The assembly in Marbel has marvelous possibilities."[1]

On his second trip to Mindanao, he saw the island as "a field of wonderful opportunities." He pointed out the growing communities because of settlers coming by the thousands every month, yet he noted that there was no evangelical church in many of the settlements. In some places, Protestant settlers had built their own churches while waiting for a minister to pastor them. Esperanza appealed, "The need is great; the opportunity for service is tremendous. Pray that the Lord will send laborers into His harvest field."[2]

His visionary gift served the PGCAG well as he was not content with the status quo but kept pressing on to see his vision for the denomination come to pass. Esperanza's vision for the Assemblies of God in the Philippines included the following:

Church Buildings

Esperanza presented his vision of the church:

The Lord Jesus Christ had a goal in preaching. 'I will build my church and the gates of hell shall not prevail against it.' Matthew 16:18. We could not merely be evangelizing, or be establishing MISSIONS, or be bringing about a change by education or social betterment upon a people. Our goal must be to establish a New Testament Church by New Testament methods and principles.[3]

Esperanza wanted to see the gospel spread throughout the Philippines. Consequently, his desire was to see church buildings constructed all over the country to serve as beacons which would attract Filipinos to come, hear and receive the gospel, and become ready for Jesus' soon return. Perhaps because of the denomination's financial difficulties, he encouraged and appreciated pioneering pastors and congregations who used their own resources to construct their church buildings. As much as possible, he espoused indigenous principles, that churches be self-supporting, self-propagating, and self-governing.

In February 1949, he pointed out various church buildings in San Nicolas and Dingras, Ilocos Norte, which were either under construction or had been completed at members' own expense.[4]

The congregation of Villasis, Pangasinan, was likewise busy building a new church. Pozorrubio's Pentecostal Church was getting ready to build a house of worship on its own lot.[5] Pastor Collado's congregation in Marbel, Cotabato, was building a church right in town. In the light of this, he appealed, "Let us pray for the others that God will supply their needs to build their new churches."[6]

In postwar Mindanao, he commended the few pioneers who had left their own provinces and went to a strange land with "God-born daring faith," "blazing a trail, breaking ground and sowing the seed of eternal life in the midst of trials and difficulties." Esperanza considered Mindanao "a challenge in missionary endeavor." Thus, the fact that, despite great hindrances, some local congregations forged ahead in building their churches on their own lots using sturdy materials was truly worthy of commendation.[7]

On May 12, 1949, as church buildings were being constructed in northern Luzon and Mindanao, Esperanza attended the dedication service of the AG church in Dueñas, Iloilo, in the Visayas. Pastor Eugenio Suede spearheaded the construction of the church, the only Protestant church in their *poblacion* (town proper).[8] The pastor of the Foursquare church attended the dedication service and the Baptist choir sang a special song. The whole *poblacion* was invited to the luncheon after the dedication service and even the provincial governor graced the occasion.[9]

The prestige gained by the Dueñas church was noteworthy since at that time AG churches were little-known and usually located on what Javier has called "the wrong side of the tracks."[10] Assemblies of God church buildings were often erected in remote areas far from the center of town. Esperanza recognized the greater influence of a church in its community if the building was located in the town center. Thus, he urged everyone to pray that churches would be able to obtain lots in the center of town.[11]

With the creation of the Home Missionary Fund, which made loans available for the purchase of church lots and the construction of church buildings, church construction was accelerated. Some churches made of light materials were remodeled or reconstructed with the aid of loans from the Fund. Reconstruction using sturdy material was important since numerous tropical storms visit the archipelago every year. Many churches had financial struggles, but Esperanza exhorted them, "We have difficulties in our small congregation toward the support of a pastor, but God will always provide the needs for better churches to trusting, daring congregations."[12]

Education and Training Venues

From the start, the pioneers saw that they needed a place to train Pentecostal workers, since there was no Pentecostal Bible school in the Philippines at that time. "The training of workers baptized in the Holy Spirit has been a fundamental part of the Assemblies of God missiology almost from its inception."[13]

Bethel Bible Institute

Thus, less than two years after the PDCAG's organizational convention, a Bible school (later called Bethel Bible Institute) was opened on August 1, 1941, in Baguio City, with Leland Johnson and Esperanza in charge.[14] Soon other AG missionaries who had had to leave the turmoil in China came to help the Bible school and to study the Chinese language, hoping to return to China someday. The classes were short-lived, however. Before dawn of December 8, 1941, the Japanese air force bombed the US Navy base in Pearl Harbor, Hawaii. They then proceeded to bomb the

US military bases in Luzon in the Philippines. The US declared war against Japan, and the Philippines was caught in the middle of World War II. On December 27, Baguio City fell into Japanese hands, and all foreigners, including the Johnsons and other AG missionaries, were interned in concentration camps. The Americans remained in captivity until February 1945 when they were brought back to the US for a joyous reunion with their families.[15]

After the war, the local pastors lost no time in reviving the Bible school. However, perhaps due to the extensive damage sustained by Baguio City and by roads up to that mountain city, the school was transferred to Pozorrubio, Esperanza's hometown. Esperanza's family helped as much as they could to get the school up and running. Some buildings were put up, and the Esperanzas vacated their house and converted it to a girls' dorm. Pozorrubio's Pentecostal Church, the church that Esperanza had pioneered, was used as the school chapel. Esperanza served as the principal. The school stayed in Pozorrubio for one year, then, in 1948, it was moved to Malinta, Polo, Bulacan, closer to Manila and more centrally located in the country.[16] Before the transfer, Edwin and Oneida Brengle had come to BBI with their three children. Edwin Brengle served as BBI principal and was the driving force in establishing BBI in its new location.[17]

Other Bible Training Schools

One Bible school in Bulacan was definitely insufficient to provide enough pastors for the PDCAG's growth and expansion. Thus, with Esperanza's full support, pastors and missionaries serving in other parts of the country put up their own short-term training schools. In 1950, Warren and Marjorie Denton and Pedro and Matilde Masuecos started a 6-week training and intensive Bible study program for the workers in Antique and the rest of Panay Island.[18] The following year, forty-five students received certificates for attending a short-term Bible school in Tuding, Benguet, conducted by Floyd and Louise Horst and Trinidad Esperanza, Rudy's sister, who had also graduated from BBI.[19]

More training schools were established. In September 1951, Esperanza taught for two weeks in a Rural Training School in Isabela. Twenty students graduated, fourteen male and six female.[20] Even local churches conducted their own Bible training. In 1953, the Ilocano churches of the Luzon District Council put up a Bible school temporarily located in Sta. Maria, Ilocos Sur. They started with sixteen students.

In Iloilo City in Panay, the Iloilo Bethel Temple experienced phenomenal growth under the pastorate of Gunder and Doris Olsen. With the help of visiting evangelists like Ralph Byrd and Hal Herman, hundreds were converted, with many of them receiving the baptism in the Holy Spirit. By 1956, Sunday school attendance reached 700 in the main church and as many as 3,000 in the Sunday schools held in many outstations around the city. These Sunday school classes were handled by the church's young people, the Christ's Ambassadors (CA), who were trained in the church and then challenged to apply what they had learned in actual ministry.[21]

Still, the need for workers was growing faster than the various Bible schools and training centers could graduate them. In his Superintendent's report at the PDCAG's Tenth Annual Convention, Esperanza made this appeal:

> We look to the Bible School to supply the need of workers. The rate of the present turn out of graduates could not meet the growing needs in carrying this

Gospel of Power to the places I mentioned to you. Something must be done.

May I reiterate what I had mentioned last year that worthy young people who feel the call of God to the ministry must be encouraged to come to Bethel Bible Institute. If that young person has no means of maintenance, the congregation can take the responsibility unselfishly in the name of the Lord Jesus Christ for His glory. I propose that this could be a program by our local assemblies. I believe Bible School is the short cut way to the preparation and development of our worker.[22]

A pastor in Sogod, Southern Leyte, was converted to Pentecostalism and decided to bring his independent Bible school into the Assemblies of God. He invited Edwin Brengle over and soon Brengle was involved in establishing a Bible school, Immanuel Bible Institute.[23] When classes started in 1953, IBI had 31 students. Some of them were BBI students from the Visayas who were grateful that they no longer needed to make the long trip to Manila for their Bible training.[24] However, Cebu City was more central in the Visayas than Sogod, Leyte. Thus, when a typhoon damaged the Bible school buildings in Sogod, the Brengles looked for a better location in Cebu City and once again started building. By the time the new IBI property was dedicated on October 7, 1955, the school already had two batches of graduates.[25]

Esperanza gave attention to the support of Filipino Bible school teachers. He knew Filipino teachers were vital to the training of Filipino workers. Thus, he led the Council in passing a resolution for the support of national teachers at BBI, the recognized District school at that time. Also, he gave attention to the upgrading of pastors. The big BBI campus in Malinta became the venue not only for the District's annual conventions but also for the Ministers Institute. The first meeting was held January 2-5, 1950. Pastors gathered for teaching and also times of spiritual refreshing. The Ministers Institute became an annual activity and was later held in various venues.

Various Regional Schools

Slowly but surely, Esperanza's vision for more Bible training for the AG's constituents took shape and grew. When the denomination became an independent General Council and the country was divided into districts, regional Bible schools were established. By 1966, the PGCAG had Bethel Bible Institute (BBI) in Manila, Immanuel Bible Institute (IBI) in Cebu, Luzon Bible Institute (LBI) in Pangasinan, Assemblies of God Bible Institute of Mindanao (AGBIM) in General Santos, and the newly established South Central Bible Institute (SCBI) in Bicol. It was also under Esperanza's watch when the USAG spearheaded the putting up of Far East Advanced School of Theology (FEAST) [now known as the Asia Pacific Theological Seminary and located in Baguio City, Philippines], the AG graduate level theological institute serving the Far East. Manila was chosen as the best location for FEAST. Thus, the FEAST building was constructed inside the BBI campus. In a report published in the *Pentecostal Voice*, the PGCAG's official magazine back then, Maynard Ketcham, the USAG Field Secretary for the Far East, reported, "The Philippines is possibly the fastest growing field in the area. The four Bible schools are filled to capacity—nearly one hundred students per school. A new 'post graduate' school is now established and Filipino brethren are using local resources to bring into being an additional Bible school."[26]

Sunday School

Esperanza's vision in the field of education and training went beyond Bible schools. He saw the church's Sunday school program as vital to establishing new converts in AG doctrine. When the District Council reconvened after the war, he pushed for a Sunday school convention. He deplored the weak support given to this vital church program.

> During our last Annual Meeting, we planned to have a Sunday school convention to lay out a program that suits our local conditions in the promotion of our Sunday school work. We are so sorry we failed to do this.
>
> We are commonly guilty of having this essential work merely marginal in our church program...It must not be forgotten that the church has a teaching mission...Our new converts or believers fresh from heathendom or rescued from Roman Catholicism and ignorance of the Word of God, must be indoctrinated, for he [sic] is surrounded with false teachings, auguries and divinations of the Filipino life. It is the Sunday school that affords them the blessed opportunity.[27]

It took some time for Esperanza's call to be heeded. The Sunday School Department was finally created in the 1951 annual convention.[28] Two years later, the first Regional Sunday School Convention was held at the Tuding AG Church, in Tuding, Benguet, on January 30 and 31. However, it would take a few more years before a national convention would be held.[29]

Pentecostal Schools

Esperanza's vision in education extended further still, to another frontier. In the 1966 convention, a resolution was passed encouraging churches to open kindergarten schools. The following year, Esperanza reported that a few churches had started. Two groups even planned to establish secondary schools. "It seems that it is high time for us to venture into the field of education," he commented.[30] In fact, Esperanza himself planned to do the same. Gumallaoi recounts a conversation he had with Esperanza shortly before the latter passed away: "'I tell you these plans,' he told me. 'I bought that part of land, the east part of the Sabatan...I will put up a Pentecostal high school.' That was his dream then, to put up a Pentecostal high school in that place. But he died before he could do this."[31]

Many AG pastors picked up the baton Esperanza left when he passed away. Bethel Bible College (BBC) has been running a vibrant preschool for many years. My son attended the preschool run by Immanuel Bible College (IBC). That preschool expanded to an elementary school before it closed. Many AG churches now run their own preschools. Quite a few have elementary schools, and some even offer up to high school. Thus, many young Filipino students hear the Pentecostal gospel before they reach their teen years. This is what Esperanza envisioned.

PGCAG Headquarters Building

After the war, the PDCAG headquarters was in Pozorrubio, where BBI was. This was probably due to the fact that Esperanza was head of both the District and BBI at that time. The Bible school moved to its new campus in Malinta in 1948, and the headquarters followed a year later. It moved for the same reason as the Bible school: Manila was centrally located and best served the needs of the whole PDCAG.[32]

At the start, when the District became a General Council, the executive officers held office in their residences.[33] Later, the PGCAG headquarters in Manila was housed in rented rooms in Manila Bethel Temple.[34] However, having a separate general headquarters building that would service the needs of the General Council was a primary vision of Esperanza.[35] To him, that headquarters building would symbolize the denomination's unity and strength, "a unity and strength in the Holy Spirit of a people desirous of directing their own religious destiny under the guidance and leadership of their Lord Jesus Christ."[36]

It took a long time, but his dream slowly came to fruition. With great joy, he made the following announcement during the 1967 General Council convention:

> Our search for a place to construct our headquarters building ended when the General Council of the Assemblies of God U.S.A. through the chairman of the Philippines Field Fellowship, Rev. Derrick Hillary, gave us a portion of the property of Bethel Bible Institute west of the BBI road and along the barrio Malinta-Malabon road, with an area of 620 sq. meters. This lot is given to us free, Praise the Lord!...We enjoin, therefore, that all Districts and all churches and every individual of our fellowship must support and contribute to the building of our Headquarters which will be a visible monument of our spirit of true cooperative fellowship.[37]

The construction of the building required several stages, however. The first groundbreaking for the PGCAG headquarters was done under Esperanza's watch. Construction had to wait while the denomination raised funds. After Esperanza died, the denomination was soon immersed in internal strife and legal disputes that lasted for many years. The headquarters project was placed on the back burner. It was not until Eli Javier became General Superintendent that another groundbreaking was held at the corner of the entrance to the BBI campus. Metal posts were laid, but construction was discontinued, probably due to insufficient funds.

Finally, during the period when Javier was on leave, his assistant, David Sobrepeña, spearheaded the construction of the headquarters at the present location. It was intended to erect the building at the site of the first groundbreaking, but the final structure only covered part of the area.[38] The General Headquarters building was finally dedicated on April 30, 1996. Signatories on the inauguration marker were Eleazer Javier, General Superintendent and President; David Sobrepeña, Assistant General Superintendent and Vice President; Felipe Acena, General and Corporate Secretary; Carmelita Gallardo, General and Corporate Treasurer; William Snider, Assembly of God Missionary Fellowship Chairman; and Anacleto Lobarbio, Southern Tagalog District Council Superintendent.

Esperanza never saw the building that he had envisioned, but he passed on his vision to others who brought it to fruition.

Literature Publication

From the beginning of the Assemblies of God's work in the Philippines, Filipino pioneers recognized the importance of good literature.[39] Assemblies of God missionaries who came to the Philippines made great use of literature to reach Filipinos with the gospel.[40] The Caudles used gospel tracts and copies of the *Pentecostal Evangel* to open doors for witnessing.[41] The Warren Dentons held public meetings during market days in the various towns of Antique. After the meetings, they gave away tracts, copies of the *Pentecostal Evangel*, and other literature so that people could take the gospel message home with them.⁴²

Official Publishing Organ

The role of the printed page is prominent in sources dealing with the early Pentecostal movement in the USA. Various groups became well-known because they had their own magazine or newspaper regularly sent out to supporters or subscribers. For instance, David Daniels III says that the *Apostolic Faith* greatly helped in giving the Azusa Movement, under William J. Seymour, crucial early leadership.⁴³ The importance of the magazines becomes clearer when we note that groups whose magazines failed either declined in numbers or disbanded altogether. Robert Owens writes that when Clara Lum and Florence Crawford left with the mailing lists of the *Apostolic Faith*, "the Azusa Street Mission was effectively cut off from its worldwide support and soon lost its resources and influence."⁴⁴

Showing the same thrust, the first literature project of the PDCAG was an official organ, the *Bulletin*. It served as the vehicle for inspiring AG constituents and communicating the leadership's vision to their members. Through his regular column, Esperanza reported on his various activities as Superintendent, announced forthcoming activities of the denomination, and appealed for people to support various projects. He also contributed articles on various topics regarding AG doctrines and polity.

The *Bulletin* began publication before the war, but the editorial staff had to evacuate when the war broke out. It was revived after the liberation, with the first issue coming out in January 1947.⁴⁵ In the 1956 General Council Convention, it was renamed the *Pentecostal Voice*. A newly formed Literature Committee made plans to improve the magazine and to generate more support from AG pastors and churches.⁴⁶ Despite these efforts, however, at some point in the early 1970s, publication of the magazine was discontinued.⁴⁷ Through the years, there have been several attempts to come up with another official organ. With the development of the internet, the denomination's official website has been fulfilling the functions of the *Bulletin* and its successors.

Ilocano Song Books

Filipinos love to express themselves through music. Songs are also effective tools for teaching doctrines and values. Moreover, as Sanneh declares, "[T]ranslations stimulated cultural pride."⁴⁸ Believing in the influence of songs in the lives of Filipinos, Esperanza led the 1949 District convention in the creation of a Song Book Committee that would compose and arrange Christian songs in Ilocano.⁴⁹ The following year, the song books were ready for sale to Ilocano-speaking AG constituents, with the belief that, in addition to providing a uniform song book for the churches, it would also bolster the spirit of Pentecostal fellowship among the brethren.⁵⁰ Note that most of the Filipino pioneers who came back from the US were from northern Luzon. A smaller number came from the Visayas.⁵¹ Consequently, by the April 1951 General District Council Convention, Esperanza reported that AG churches were found only in Isabela, Ilocos Norte, Ilocos Sur, Abra, La Union, Mountain Province, Pangasinan and Tarlac, i.e., mostly in northern Luzon, among Ilocano-speakers. In the Visayas, the AG churches were primarily among the locals in Panay and Southern Leyte. In Mindanao, the work was confined to Cotabato.⁵² No church was as yet established in the Tagalog regions. It was not until later in 1951, when Paul and Violet Pipkin pioneered the Glad Tidings Evangelistic Center (later

Bethel Temple) in Manila, that an AG church was established among the Tagalogs.[53] Thus, since the denomination's headquarters and Bible school were initially in northern Luzon, resources were more readily available for the Ilocano area. As a result, Ilocano song books were published first.

Local Sunday School and Bible Study Materials

Early on, AG churches in the Philippines were using back-dated Sunday school quarterlies from the US. Soon requests came for local quarterlies to be published regularly.[54] Moreover, the District saw the need for teaching materials written in new converts' dialects. Since most of the pioneer churches were located away from town centers, many converts were ordinary citizens with little education and could barely speak English. Requests came from Ilocano-speaking sections for Bible study materials in their dialect. Under Esperanza's leadership, the District chose to translate P. C. Nelson's *Bible Doctrines*, a standard AG doctrinal text, into Ilocano.[55] The translations were mimeographed and sold chapter by chapter as each chapter's translation was completed. Used as Sunday school materials, these gave new AG converts the basics of the doctrinal stand of the Assemblies of God.[56]

As with the local song books, early translations of Bible study materials were in Ilocano. In fact, the first dialect articles to be included in the *Bulletin* were in Ilocano. With the District headquarters and Bible school initially located in an Ilocano-speaking area, and with the PDCAG's organizational convention held in the same area, naturally the majority of the denomination's leaders were Ilocano speakers. Consequently, requests from the Ilocano-speaking congregations reached the leadership faster and were given greater attention. However, other dialects were not entirely neglected. Later, Cebuano, Ilonggo, and Tagalog materials were also printed.

With all of the requests for materials in the local dialects coming in, in 1952, Esperanza presented the "necessity of having a board of translators to translate the English S.S. materials and Correspondence Bible Courses into the major dialects to fully benefit the people." He recognized that this would entail discovering and utilizing the District's best talents and pooling together financial resources to fund the translation work. Yet these were worthy investments to strengthen the constituents and help train workers.[57]

By 1965, more than a decade later, the need for translators was still great. Esperanza published another call for "native talents who will be able to interpret and transcribe into our own Filipino way of thought and life the Gospel Truths." The Council already recognized the need for contextualization: "We must not be just translators of Gospel literatures extracted from American thinkers but print full gospel and Pentecostal literatures product of Filipino Spirit-filled Teachers."[58] Filipino Pentecostals were beginning to express Pentecostal doctrine using Filipino concepts more readily understood by their constituents.

Drawing a lesson from Communist elements that were by then infiltrating Philippine society, Esperanza observed that propaganda through the printed page was the Communists' "most powerful and effective weapon for influencing, conditioning and manipulating people." He believed that if the Communists could win converts through the printed page, so could Spirit-filled Christians writing potent and dynamic articles intended to spread the gospel. He stressed, "We need such Gospel materials that will fortify the mind of the youngest and oldest in our churches and in our Sunday School. We need Gospel literature that will be like [a] wall of faith strengthening each member in the Lord, providing him with effective tools for reaching the lost."⁵⁹

Evangel Press

The expanded publication of gospel literature reinforced the need to acquire printing equipment. The Evangel Press played a major role in this endeavor. At the start, the *Bulletin* and other materials were prepared using an ordinary typewriter, then printed with a mimeograph machine and, later, a Gestetner duplicating machine.⁶⁰ Floyd Horst, an AG missionary in the Philippines, sensed God directing him in literature production. At that time, the denomination's printing needs were serviced by commercial presses, which followed their own production schedules and not the denomination's deadlines. Moreover, Horst realized that any profit gained by commercial presses could have gone to printing more gospel literature. Thus, when the Horsts returned to the Philippines from furlough in 1955, they brought with them two hand-fed letterpresses. That was the start of Evangel Press.⁶¹ From the beginning, Esperanza encouraged the project and extended whatever help he could. With the cooperative efforts of the PDCAG, the Philippine Field Fellowship (PFF)—the organization of USAG missionaries in the Philippines—and friends from the US, three Speed the Light offset presses were purchased. Later, an Evangel Press building was constructed to house the printing equipment.⁶²

In 1967, Ketcham reported that a "super" press had been ordered from Sweden. Its arrival would make Evangel Press "the largest Assemblies of God printing establishment in the Far East and soon...one of the largest in world-wide Assemblies of God mission circles."⁶³

Despite the progress in technology, however, one problem plagued the literature and publication programs of the

PDCAG/PGCAG from the start—the lack of support from AG constituents in buying the magazines and other materials being published. In her report at the PDCAG's 1951 Annual Convention, *Bulletin* editor Trinidad Esperanza, who received no compensation for her work, informed the convention of the financial challenges the District organ was facing due to rapidly rising prices of materials and postage. She asked the District for help. She also asked that the paper's subscription rate be increased.[64] For several successive years, both the *Bulletin* editor and the General Superintendent repeatedly urged AG pastors and members to support the organ with their subscriptions. When the *Bulletin* was later renamed the *Pentecostal Voice*, the magazine's publishers came out with various promotion strategies to encourage subscription, though apparently with little response. Later, Calvin Zeissler, chairman of the Philippines Literature Committee and, soon after, head of Evangel Press, diligently promoted the importance of literature through his regular column in the *Pentecostal Voice*. He, too, repeatedly solicited the support of the readers. Below is one of his appeals:

> At the same time, while in the midst of progress, we have seen a decline in other areas. This is true of our Sunday School publications. At present we are publishing Adult Student quarterlies in the major dialects, and the total orders per quarter have not been sufficient to cover the cost of printing and therefore we are losing money every time. Unless our churches will be faithful in ordering this material, we may be forced to stop printing....Evangel Publishers can be successful and a help to you only if you will be loyal and faithful to support its ministry by ordering and making use of the materials it has available for you. Our prices are the lowest we can possibly make. This can only be so if we receive enough orders.[65]

Recognizing the reluctance of the Filipinos to purchase their own AG publications, Esperanza made this plea:

> To make our program pay for itself, we must patronize our locally produced literature and promote them. In short, we must buy them and pay for them and sell them to others.
>
> The PENTECOSTAL VOICE needs your patronage and promotion. This is our paper. Let us make it a paper as we hope it to be.⁶⁶

The plea obviously went unheeded. Publication of the *Pentecostal Voice* was discontinued. An item in the report of the Philippines Literature Committee at the 1959 General Council Convention lists some of the problems plaguing the paper:

> At the Literature Committee meeting of July 21, 1957, the Voice fell to the hand of Brother Esperanza—almost like an unwanted orphan child. Many problems, no news to print, no funds or hands for printing, many debts from those who had not paid for bundles of copies sent to them, falling lists of subscription. A patient with a fatal achness [sic], each fatal by itself.⁶⁷

It is interesting to note that on the same page of the report was this note: "During the absence of Brother Horst, the Literature Committee approved that Brother Esperanza will manage Evangel Book Room and Evangel Press." It seems that the Literature Committee passed on to Esperanza some of the problems that it could not handle. Esperanza seemed to have had no choice but to accept this task that no one else wanted.

Later, Evangel Press itself was closed down for various reasons, among which were "a backlog of unpaid bills for ordered literature" and the fact that Filipinos did not perceive the Press as their own but belonging to the missionaries.⁶⁸ Perhaps Filipino AG churches had become used to free literature, whether from the AG or other organizations. Perhaps church finances were so tight that other priorities pushed the purchase of Christian literature out of the budget. Perhaps it was a combination of both, plus other factors unique to each church. Whatever the extenuating circumstances may have been, one thing for sure was that publication of the official organ was discontinued due to financial difficulties. The USAG had to step in and help, as was usually the case when the denomination was in dire need of finances. Presently, the PGCAG is working hand-in-hand with the International Correspondence Institute (ICI) and Asia Pacific Media Ministries (APMM) to meet its publication needs.⁶⁹

Radio Programs

Esperanza saw the radio as a powerful tool for evangelism, so he led the AG in sponsoring radio programs.⁷⁰ As early as 1949, he led the school's faculty and students in producing *Bethel Hour*, a half-hour radio program aired over DZAS, operated by the Far East Broadcasting Company (FEBC), every Saturday, 7:30 to 8:00 p.m. The program had songs, testimonies, and sermons.⁷¹ Within two years, more programs were added and aired throughout the week in English, Ilocano, and Cebuano.

Through the years, other radio programs were supported by the PGCAG. In the early 1950s, Paul and Violet Pipkin, then working with the FEBC, developed the *Sunday School of the Air*, featuring Sunday school lessons, skits, testimonies, and the Bread of Life Correspondence School, which offered 15 Bible-based lessons for the program's listeners.⁷² Names of students enrolled in the correspondence lessons were channeled to the various districts for follow-up.[73] The program became the "flag-bearer" for the Radio Evangelism Department (Philippines Radio Outreach). By 1966, the Radio Evangelism Department, by then directed by Leonard Lanphear, had greatly expanded the ministry's scope to reach the Visayas and Mindanao. Esperanza was the host of the Ilocano program, *Tinapay ti Biag* ("Bread of Life").

Several districts also came up with their own radio programs. For example, in 1967, the Christ's Ambassadors (CA) of the Assemblies of God in Marbel, Cotabato, started airing *The Christ's Ambassador Broadcast* over DXKI.[74] On February 14, 1988, the Southern Tagalog District Council (STDC) produced *Himala ng Buhay* ("Miracle of Life") aired over DWOO (now DWSS). The program is still airing as of this writing.[75] Around the 1990s, David Sobrepeña hosted *Hope for You*. This was later replaced by the Tagalog *Pag-asa Para sa 'Yo*, hosted by Peter Banzon, with Anacleto Lobarbio as speaker. In 2004, STDC took over the production of the program with the help of APMM, and it is still being broadcasted all over the country as of this writing.[76]

Pastors used the radio programs as evangelistic tools. Esperanza reported that when he and his companions visited Bangui, Ilocos Norte, they brought along a radio. Before the service started, they used the DZAS radio programs to prepare the hearts of the people to receive God's word. When the altar call was given, four women received Christ as their Savior.[77]

In the early 1950s, FEBC distributed radios, tuned only to DZAS, to various Christian churches. The radios were placed under the care of responsible church members who would use them as tools for evangelism and discipleship. They were also to submit reports to FEBC on how the radios were being used.[78] Many AG church members were recipients of the radios. A recipient from Aurora, Isabela, wrote that the radio was being passed from one member's house to another. They were all glad to be able to listen to songs, testimonies, and messages in Ilocano. They wished the Ilocano programs were aired daily.[79] Avelino Taplac, an AG pioneer, brought an FEBC radio receiver to Mindoro. When people heard he had a radio, they gathered to listen to gospel songs, testimonies, and gospel messages. Sometimes Taplac would turn off the radio to explain further the message they had just heard. He testified of people who were converted with the help of the radio.[80]

An amazing testimony to the result of radio ministry was shared by Aurelio Gonzales, the speaker for *Oras ti Naimbag a Damag* (The Good News Hour), which aired in Ilocos Norte. An Ilocano sugar plantation worker in Hawaii had been converted. When he returned to his home in a remote village at the foot of a mountain in Ilocos Norte, his only source of spiritual feeding was the radio program of Gonzales. He gathered his relatives to listen to the program, aired three times weekly. Not content with listening to the program, he visited Gonzales, taking along some relatives. He asked that a preacher come to their village to further explain the gospel to them. Gonzales promptly went, shared the gospel, and was amazed to note that the people had already learned a lot through the radio programs. At the end of the visit, thirteen converts were baptized in water. The family donated 200 square meters of their corn plantation so that a church could be constructed in their village. The church was built, the only church of any kind in that village, and an AG minister became pastor of the church.[81]

This testimony proved Esperanza's declaration that radio programs penetrated into Filipino homes regardless of religious affiliation and reached houses even in remote areas.[82]

Foreign Missions

In the 1950s, C. K. Tobit, a delegate of the Indian Pentecostal Assemblies to the International Pentecostal Conference in Paris, France, visited several countries, including the Philippines, on her way back to India. Esperanza hosted her for a month while she ministered at the Bible school and other places in the country. Esperanza was impressed when she said that Indian nationals were realizing their responsibility to bring the gospel to their own people and to people of other lands. Esperanza issued the following challenge to Filipinos: "May it be the God-given burden of our hearts, as Nationals, to reach our own people and to have missionary vision beyond our shores."[83] However, the needs and concerns of the growing denomination, plus the internal conflicts that the PGCAG leadership sought to resolve, left little time or resources for the needs of other lands.

Finally, at the 1965 General Council Convention, PGCAG's Silver Jubilee celebration, Esperanza spoke:

> We have been talking so much and so long of Foreign Missions. We created a Missions Department but little is being done for missions. We sing: 'Christ is the Answer' but we limit this only to Filipinos. Let us begin dedicating ourselves to MISSIONS and begin to send out of the Philippines a couple, at least, to a foreign soil. This is the will of God for the Assemblies of God in the Philippines. God will smile at us if we make this sacrifice, and initial step.[84]

At that same convention, a resolution was passed in support of the Council's foreign missions program:

> Whereas, inasmuch that we are making a new move of faith to send missionaries outside the Philippines, it is strongly recommended that each organized church give at least ₱2.00 or more each month as offering for the Foreign Mission Fund.

It was clarified that this amount was in addition to the regular monthly missions offering.[85]

With the General Superintendent's active endorsement of foreign missions, the constituents of the General Council followed suit. BBI boosted the foreign missions drive by focusing on foreign missions in its third annual missions convention, held September 28-29, 1965.[86] The following year, the Southern Luzon District (presently STDC) held the first missions rally, noted as "one of the boldest and most aggressive moves ever yet conceived and undertaken" by a district. The rally was so successful that the District's sections held their own missions rallies.

The *Pentecostal Voice* gave the rallies full-page treatment with the following comment:

> These rallies in this district may yet become the starting point for a nation-wide move among all Assemblies of God churches to take part actively in the missionary program of the [PGCAG]. The dwindling interest of sending missionaries abroad among ministers and members which has its beginning during the last General Council Convention was given a booster shot in the arm by these new moves in the Southern Luzon District.[87]

Pentecostal Voice editor Solomon Balimbin added his voice to the rising chorus calling for the Council's greater involvement in foreign missions. He urged Council leaders to be more proactive:

The Assemblies of God in the Philippines is also preparing to send missionaries. But at the rate she is pushing this program, it will be an accomplishment if she can send one missionary couple in two years....

Any effort, no matter what it is, depends upon the leader. If the leader fails, the project fails. On the other hand, if the leader will exert all his effort, and with the help of God, that project is bound to succeed. Our missionary program needs the full cooperation of our leaders. It needs their whole heart, their time, effort and attention. If the leaders will not give their wholehearted effort to this project, well, we can predict the outcome of our missionary program.[88]

In its May 1967 issue, the magazine ran the article, "Every Christian a Missionary," stressing that every Christian was responsible to carry the gospel to those within his/her reach, whether at home or abroad.[89]

One proactive step the Council took was to send Rev. Eliseo Sadorra, the Assistant General Superintendent and Missions Director, to the Asia-South Pacific Congress on Evangelism, held in Singapore, November 5-13, 1968. Sadorra met with AG representatives from various Asian countries and discussed the possibility of their accommodating Filipino AG missionaries in their countries. AG heads from India, Pakistan, Taiwan, and Japan expressed an urgent need for Filipino missionaries. Sadorra also visited Vietnam, Singapore, Indonesia, Malaysia, Thailand, and Hong Kong to see firsthand Missions' needs in each country. Wherever he went, he received positive responses to the plan to send Filipino missionaries.[90]

At Esperanza's last General Council Convention, the speaker was Rev. Paul Schoch, pastor of the leading missionary church of the Northern California-Nevada District and fourth-highest missions-giving church of the Assemblies of God in the US.[91] Most probably as planned, "from the beginning up to the end of the convention, people were so challenged to support missions." Esperanza spoke the first night of the convention. When he made an appeal for missions, the congregation responded by giving ₱1,100 in just one night.[92]

In his annual report to the body, once more he stressed missions:

> To live is to die to ourselves. Natural and spiritual laws tell us that to multiply one must go through the process of death. "Except a grain of wheat falleth to the ground and die, it abideth alone." In order to multiply we must die to ourselves. Missions, domestic and [f]oreign, can be realized only through dying to our own. The facilities and framework of our organization provide vehicles in carrying out this principle. We are an evangelistic and missionary body. We can give through the energy of the Holy Spirit life to the extent of our dying to ourselves and being alive in the Lord. Missions means giving ourselves and all our resources to the unfinished task. This is not the concern of the Stewardship Department only. It is the purpose of our existence, to continue His work, and in the dynamics of the Holy Spirit.[93]

Esperanza's passion to send out Filipino missionaries drove him to volunteer to head the Council's Missions Department after he was reelected in the 1969 General Council Convention. He believed, "Now is the time to send some young men and women to the harvest field."[94]

Pursuant to his own words, Esperanza visited Samuel and Deborah Onggao Lazaro, who were teaching at IBI in Cebu, to inform the couple that he was sending them to Guam as missionaries. He eagerly worked on the Lazaros' travel papers. However, he passed away before he could complete the travel requirements. For this reason , the Lazaros were not able to go to Guam as missionaries.[95]

Esperanza's life was the grain of wheat that fell to the ground and died—but multiplied. By the year 2000, the PGCAG had sent fifteen cross-cultural missionaries overseas.[96] Presently, the PGCAG World Missions Department holds the Institute of Missions Basics (IMB) for those preparing for foreign missions ministry. IMB graduates are channeled to the Department's Project Barnabas, which aids PGCAG-commissioned missionaries.[97]

With a broad sweep of Esperanza's visionary leadership and accomplishments firmly in view, the next chapter will present a historical assessment of the impact of his life and leadership upon the PGCAG.

Chapter 9

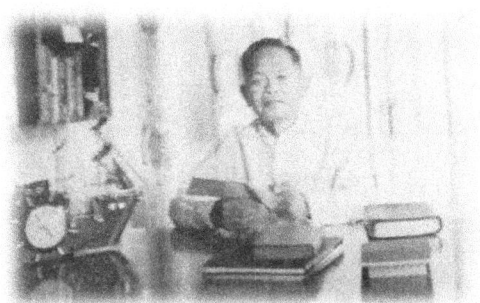

Esperanza at his office
Source: Esperanza Collection, Asia Pacific Research Center, APTS, Baguio City

ASSESSMENT OF ESPERANZA'S LEADERSHIP ROLE AND INFLUENCE

Rudy Esperanza served the PDCAG/PGCAG from 1940 to 1969, almost three decades. The only other General Superintendent who has served more than a decade is Eli Javier, from 1977 to 1997. Javier sums up Esperanza's vision as follows:

> [D]uring those days, hardly do people speak of vision as we do now. Visions then were like dreams. But, if what I recall is right, he was really intending to let the Assemblies of God cover the whole Philippines....So he was on the go....He was a good model, working his best with very limited resources; limited resources in terms of man power, and money, and materials. To me that is a part of good leadership: doing much with little, because many leaders can do grand things because they have plenty of resources and even connections....To me that is very significant, a leader doing much with little.[1]

Rudy Esperanza was a visionary. He saw beyond what was before him to what could be. Then he gave his all to see what he had envisioned come to pass. As he loved to do, he planted, so that the present PGCAG generation could enjoy the fruits of his labor.

Forging Unity

Finally, this book will be remiss if it does not point out one of Esperanza's major underlying motivation as he pursued his various roles in the PGCAG. He aimed to forge a united PGCAG. Each of his annual reports kept in the PGCAG archives includes a call for unity. Below are some examples:

> 1952 – Tenth PDCAG Annual Convention: 'The urgency of the hour necessitates the pooling of our efforts and resources together in unselfish service, devotion and love to the Master. Let us work with all we have, careful of consciences and careless of our lives, and be conquerors for Jesus, showing forth indeed that we have been born from above, citizens of another world. Let us work while it is day; the night is coming when no man can work.'[2]
>
> 1963 – Fifth PGCAG General Council Convention: 'We must not only work, but work together. Our love and devotion to the Lord must drive us to united action. Let us close rank and give no opportunity to the enemy's divisive power.'[3]
>
> 1965 – Sixth General Council Convention, Silver Jubilee of PGCAG: 'We are so thankful to our God for this another opportunity as representative and component parts of the Body of Christ, the habitation of God in the Spirit, to display as one Fellowship the inherent principles of unity, fellowship, cooperation, equality and love....I also

trust that in our gathering together like this, we are deepen [sic] conscious of our common collective responsibility and view the past with praise and thanksgiving to God with a wider platitude of togetherness in the many varied aspects and facets of the work each of us seem to be doing out of unity. May we be deepened with conviction in our responsibility to be faithful to the leadership the Holy Spirit has raised among us....We are here together to seek the Lord and implore His direction and help relative to the work God has entrusted to us together to do. We are here to counsel together binding ourselves in the unity of faith and purpose in the bond of peace and love to the glory of God.'[4]

1967 – Seventh PGCAG General Council Convention: 'There is no real cooperation but voluntary cooperation. There is no true fellowship but cooperative fellowship. There is no real fellowship but in love. Let us move forward and advance as one body and organism in Christ, binding ourselves in the same principles as we declared in our Constitution and By-Laws.'[5]

1969 – Eighth PGCAG General Council Convention. The key word in this report is 'togetherness.' The pastors' failure to submit to the Treasurer a required report assessing the denomination's net worth and land holdings was a 'failure in togetherness.' Participating in the missions program was a 'profitable area of togetherness.' The *Pentecostal Voice* needed the people's support; it needed the people's togetherness. He called for everyone to 'exemplify togetherness in the realm of evangelism.'

He closed his report with this illustration: "Our togetherness is vital and essential. We cannot be a good 'walis' [broom] by standing alone. We cannot do the job. It takes us all together bound by the common purpose and love of the Master that we can achieve."[6]

Esperanza often ended his report by saying, "Yours in His fellowship" or "Yours in His loving fellowship" or simply "In His fellowship." He was obviously stressing to the AG constituents that the PGCAG was a "voluntary cooperative fellowship" needing everyone to "show or demonstrate this spirit by assuming full responsibilities of voluntary affiliation to the fellowship."[7] The term "cooperative fellowship" was actually taken from the PGCAG Constitution and Bylaws preamble, which is basically the same as the preamble of the General Council of the Assemblies of God, USA.[8] It has the same basic emphasis on unity. Putting the preamble into practice, however, was easier said than done. Esperanza faced this task as he sought to guide the PGCAG along a united path. His task was to unite Filipinos with each other and with the American missionaries who had come to work side-by-side with local pastors in spreading the gospel among Filipinos.

The USAG pioneers faced the challenge of unifying ministers coming from varied theological backgrounds and religious affiliations. Negative experiences in their previous church groups were "baggage" carried over to the new denomination, weighing down efforts to press forward as one. Added to the challenge was the fact that some of the pioneering members were already leaders of their own Pentecostal groups and were used to being obeyed by their followers. PGCAG leaders had to contend with the same challenges in uniting Filipino AG pioneers, but cultural hindrances to unity made the task even more difficult.

As in a marriage, the first years of the AG in the Philippines were a "honeymoon stage" of harmonious fellowship, although it was interrupted by World War II. The pastors regrouped in 1946. In his 1950 report, Esperanza observed, "There is a growing spirit of cooperation and united effort and love in the fellowship. It has been our prayer always that this will be the peculiar mark of our fellowship and that nothing will destroy this love and unity. We may be tried, tested and hindered but may this unity and love continue to increase in spiritual sacrifice."[9]

The AG's focus back then was growth and expansion. Esperanza lamented the fact that, aside from northern Luzon, the AG work was limited to Panay and Leyte, with some pioneers trying to open work in Cebu and Mindoro. Work in Mindanao was limited to Cotabato. There was none in other parts of Luzon.[10] Workers were urged to focus on the vast unfinished task ahead. However, while everyone seemed to be busy evangelizing, dark clouds of contention were beginning to gather over the denomination.

In 1953, the District Council passed a resolution to become a General Council independent of the mother organization in the US. The reason given for the resolution was the growth of the PDCAG throughout the archipelago.[11] However, in the next General Council Convention, Esperanza stated the real reason behind the resolution for independence:

> Three years ago, we were gathered in Malinta, Polo, Bulacan, faced with some kind of divisive problem that was spurred by the spirit of more regional supervision and colored by sort of personal ambition. This was overcome in the Spirit of the Lord by availing ourselves with the convenience of the machinery of our Assembly of God polity. We had resolved to be a General Council, adopted a General Constitution and by-laws, and

divided the territory of the Philippines into three regional Districts according to the natural island groups: Luzon, Visayas and Mindanao.[12]

Based on the above report, the catalyst behind the resolution to be a General Council was a "divisive problem" coupled with "personal ambition." The regional grouping allowed people of the same dialect to choose their own leaders, instead of each group vying to put its own in top leadership positions in the denomination. However, becoming a General Council and dividing the country into three regions did not solve the problem. Carmelita Gallardo, the General Council's recording secretary for many years, recalls the conflicts between Ilocanos and Cebuanos. Later, other groups joined the fray: those from Iloilo, Pampanga, Pangasinan, and especially Ilocos, who considered themselves the "pure" Ilocanos. The regional differences were intense, preventing the groups from understanding each other.[13]

One problem among the pioneering Pentecostals in the US was the fact that young ministers gathered around strong Pentecostal leaders, producing a divisive and partisan spirit. This same problem was present among the PGCAG ministers, further complicated by regional alliances and biases.

Dumanon gives a hint of what the denomination was facing in the mid-1960s:

> Our care should not be focused alone on them outside Christ but also on those already born into the kingdom of God. For here we are faced with the problem of spiritual abnormalities. Christians born years ago remain babes in Christ. Where love should dwell, quarrels and grudges exist. Where there should be enthusiasm to preach Christ, there is the feeling of inferiority and

indifference. Where Christians should be helping others by giving, some don't even support their own church.[14]

Economic Issues

Aside from dialect groupings, another factor causing tension among pastors of the PGCAG was economics—more specifically, the tension between pastors who had their own sponsors and pastors who were dependent on their congregations for support. Various means of support were enjoyed by some Filipino AG pioneers. Many returning pastors were receiving regular financial support from friends in the US. Some American missionaries sponsored some pastors working with them in their areas of ministry. For a period of time, T. L. Osborn sponsored numerous AG pastors through his Association for Native Evangelism (ANE). These sponsors met legitimate needs, aiding the rapid spread of the gospel. However, negative side effects soon surfaced.

Instead of being loyal to the denomination, pastors gave their loyalty to benevolent sponsors, whether to another Filipino pastor, or an American missionary, or T. L. Osborn and the pastor who was the conduit of his support. The inherent Filipino value of *utang na loob* ("debt of gratitude") plays a big role in developing loyalties. Filipinos feel beholden to those who give them financial aid. These loyalties affect their choices and decisions, especially during elections. People are elected not because of their qualifications but because of their loyalties. Another negative effect was the jealousy created among pastors. When asked why the ANE support was withdrawn, Esperanza gave five reasons, the last of which was "misunderstanding between workers, or workers were jealous with one another."[15] Pastors who did not have access to sponsorships were jealous of those who did. Some pastors who were conduits of support or close to missionaries competed with each other and lorded over those beholden to them. Moreover, "Filipino pastors worked for the missionary in an employer/employee relationship," similar to the patron-laborer relationship of farming communities. Such a relationship prevented Filipinos and missionaries from reaching the ideal of working together as peers.[16] The worst scenario was when AG pastors left the denomination for a group that promised better financial support. Esperanza lamented, "Independent churches and corporations other than ourselves are in constant activities trying to build their kingdoms on foundations that were laid by pioneers of our movement."[17]

Strong Dominant Leaders

Strong leaders with dominant personalities were among the greatest challenges Esperanza faced as he strove to unite the young denomination. One issue that caused him great stress was the conflict dubbed "Battle Temple," a play on the name of Bethel Temple, the premier AG church in Manila, which was the object of the controversy.[18] Bethel Temple was a big church with many satellite churches around Manila. In fact, Bethel Temple was so prominent in the PGCAG that the problems surrounding that church negatively affected the growth of the whole denomination.[19] For many years, Bethel Temple remained the property of the USAG because its Division of Foreign Missions (DFM) required that the church's $15,000 debt should be paid before the property was transferred to the PGCAG. Thus, when Bethel Temple was embroiled in legal cases, the chairman of the Assemblies of God Missionary Fellowship (AGMF) in the Philippines was given power of attorney to represent the DFM.

In 1963, Ruben Candelaria, PGCAG General Treasurer and pastor of the Tagalog congregation of Bethel Temple, was divested of his ministerial credentials due to allegations of misappropriation of funds. Candelaria, supported by a majority of the congregation, had himself elected Administrative Pastor of the church in defiance of the PGCAG and DFM order for him to step down from his pastorate. The congregation was splintered. Some groups left Bethel Temple while others remained loyal to Candelaria. He went to court claiming that the people he represented were the real owners of Bethel Temple. He formed the "Philippine Assemblies of God" (PAG), with headquarters inside the Bethel Temple compound.[20] The DFM asked Lester Sumrall to go back to the Philippines and talk to Candelaria, who had been a close friend. However, Sumrall's mediation efforts failed. The formerly good friends parted with great animosity.

Candelaria invited Dan and Esther Marocco, former DFM missionaries in the Philippines, to work under him and pastor the English congregation. Soon, the relationship between the two men turned bitter and the congregation was again divided. Fist fights between their rival congregations led to court cases. Meanwhile, the PGCAG could no longer enter the property.

Observing Esperanza during this conflict, Javier noted that Esperanza "maintained his composure," in contrast to many around him who reacted in anger. Javier was especially impressed that despite Esperanza's great respect for Candelaria, he did not prevent the PGCAG executives from disciplining the former General Treasurer.[21]

In 1969, a government court upheld the DFM as the real owners of Bethel Temple, but Candelaria filed a motion for reconsideration. When Esperanza passed away in October of the same year, the Bethel Temple court case was still unresolved. He did not live to see the conflicts between the PGCAG and Cresencio Tandog, his Assistant General Superintendent, who took over his position and led a schism that split the whole PGCAG in 1973. He was no longer present when the DFM finally gave Bethel Temple to the PGCAG and the PGCAG decided to end the conflict by turning over Bethel Temple to David Sumrall, Lester's nephew, who had become the congregation's senior pastor. Moreover, he did not witness the joint convention in 1979 that reconciled the PGCAG with the Tandog faction.[22]

Clamor for Self-Governance

Disagreement was not only among Filipinos. As can be seen from the various conflicts described above, American missionaries were significant players in the denomination. Inevitably, tension arose between local pastors and their American counterparts.

The first American AG missionaries came to the Philippines when the country was still a protectorate of the United States. Thus, many Filipinos, especially those in the cities, were educated under the American system and could speak English well. However, the same words and actions could have entirely different meanings for Americans and Filipinos. Well-meaning words and actions could be, and were, misconstrued. To aggravate matters, Americans were perceived as following a different version of the Golden Rule: "He who has the gold makes the rules."[23] Inevitably, conflicts between American missionaries and Filipino pastors surfaced. Filipinos have a saying: *naipit sa dalawang nag-uumpugang bato* ("caught between two colliding rocks"). That was Esperanza's situation as he strove to maintain harmony between the American missionaries and the Filipino pastors.

When the Americans first came to Philippine soil, Filipino soldiers fought the US army, perceiving their erstwhile ally against the Spaniards to have colonial ambitions. This bred an undercurrent of distrust among some Filipinos towards

Americans, or any other white people. To others, however, what developed was a love-hate relationship: loving the Americans for all the help extended toward the various needs of the country and feeling beholden to them, yet hating the control and authority Americans exerted over the nationals, since for centuries, "independence was the great national ideal of the Filipino people."[24] Rejecting assimilation, no matter how benevolent, many Filipinos were clamoring for self-governance.

This desire for self-governance was another side to the controversy around Bethel Temple. Candelaria was head of the Methodists' Manila District before he joined the PGCAG. He was a seminary graduate. He felt capable to lead Manila Bethel Temple. However, the AGMF leadership obviously felt Filipinos were not yet ready to head such a big church. Thus, another missionary would be assigned as Bethel Temple's Senior Pastor whenever the post was vacated. Javier assesses the issue: "It should be noted that since 1946, the whole council had been led by Filipino nationals [i.e., Esperanza], but this was not so in the case of Bethel Temple. How long should nationals serve as associate or assistant pastors to foreign missionaries in these urban churches started by the missionaries? This became an issue. This organizational tension, related to leadership matters and to the autonomy of the local church[,] caused the schism."[25] Throughout the legal battles between the DFM[26] and Candelaria, the PGCAG stood beside the American missionaries.

Esperanza's 1963 to 1969 General Council reports do not mention the controversy surrounding Bethel Temple. Other denominations accuse Filipino Pentecostals of being triumphalistic, with a tendency to highlight the positive and hide or ignore the negative aspects of a situation. This may be true, but one also has to consider the Filipino concept of *hiya* (shame). As much as possible, Filipinos would do all they could to avoid a confrontation that would embarrass either themselves or a person they respect or value. This is related to the Filipino desire to "save face," either theirs or that of a significant other. Acting like a true Filipino with *utang na loob* towards American missionaries, Esperanza repeatedly thanked them for their various ministries in the Philippines, despite the negative undertones coming from some Filipino pastors. In response to the rising nationalistic spirit among his fellow ministers, he stressed the partnership between the Filipinos and the Americans.

That Filipinos were divided in their opinions regarding the extent of missionary involvement in denominational leadership was evident when an amendment was proposed to the Constitution's Article III, Nationals and Missionaries Relations, section 2, which states:

> That the missionaries as members of the Assemblies of God of the Philippines, shall endeavor to participate as actively as possible in all gatherings of the Assemblies of God of the Philippines, and will be willing to accept offices, *except in administrative position*, when elected.[27]

The phrase in italics is the amended portion. The minutes describe the discussion that followed:

> A motion to adopt the amendment was presented and seconded. There was a lengthy discussion between the pros and cons. Everyone like [sic] to speak for and against the amendment.
>
> A point of order was called from the floor to give chance to others to speak, until the discussion reached a hot point, and Brother Reid intervened for a few counsels [sic] and prayer.

A subsidiary motion was presented, seconded and approved to table the motion.[28]

It is interesting to note that on the same afternoon as the above heated debate, a motion was proposed that "the General Council in session express...sincere appreciation to the labor in the field and the desire for more Missionaries in the feilds [sic] where there are no Missionaries at all." The motion was unanimously approved.[29] Obviously, all wanted the missionaries to help, but not to take a top position and thus exercise control over the denomination, especially since "some missionaries were not always willing to relinquish control."[30]

Relationships between the national leaders and American missionaries took a turn for the worse in the early 1960s. On January 13, 1961, the PGCAG Executive Committee prepared a "Joint Declaration of the Filipino Brethren" in which they presented three charges against the Assemblies of God Missionary Fellowship (AGMF) in the Philippines: lack of central authority, lack of cooperation, and lack of ministry coordination. The Executive Committee then proposed measures to rectify the problems raised. The joint declaration, often referred to as the "white paper," was sent to Ketcham, who did not delay in responding. He met with the AGMF to discuss the issues raised in the declaration. In the end, Ketcham and the AGMF came up with a twenty-one point proposal for integrating the AGMF with the PGCAG.[31]

On January 30, 1968, a "Leadership and Coordination Conference" was held by Filipino General Presbytery members, District leaders, and officers of the PFF. The conference aimed to integrate the ministries of the American missionaries with the goals and ministries of the PGCAG. Moreover, it sought to help the locals and the missionaries to "progress in mutual trust and confidence."[32]

In his 1969 annual report, Esperanza informed the constituents that, as a result of the conference, the "white paper" was revised to describe how the ministry of the AGMF missionaries was integrated with the framework of the PGCAG. Copies of the revised "white paper" were made available to the constituents.

One common cause of conflict between Filipino pastors and missionaries is the issue of finance. In general, missionaries desire to help the Filipino church become truly indigenous. However, there is a delicate balance each missionary has to strive for. Derrick Hillary, AGMF Field Chairman in the late 1960s, expressed this dilemma as a question: "[H]ow...can we keep the measure of our assistance within the scope of healthy indigenous aspirations, and at the same time, not severely limit the pace of expansion we seek for God's work?" Hillary saw his question as further related to the issue of dependency and self-respect. He told the AGMF missionaries, "We must resist the temptation to keep the National Church forever obligated to, or dependent upon us. Our assistance must not be in such proportions as to preclude the possibility of the Nationals of assuming the responsibility of support from indigenous sources [sic]. Otherwise we shall embarrass and destroy respect." Dave Johnson believes that there are no simple answers to these issues, and I agree.[33]

Esperanza's Conflict Resolution Approach

How Esperanza responded to the conflicts swirling around him was a reflection of his personality and values. His way of approaching conflicts was important in gaining his constituents' trust as well as that of the missionaries, as he mediated conflicts. Above all else, it was his love for and loyalty to the PGCAG and its members that led him to sacrifice whatever was necessary for the good of the movement. His love for the people bound the PGCAG into a family despite all the cultural differences.

His humble and quiet spirit was strengthened by a singular desire to serve the needs of the PGCAG. Javier says that he did not find in Esperanza any self-serving act. "He loved the Assemblies of God. His heart was filled with a strong desire to see the movement grow and be influential even in the transformation of the Philippines."[34] A former AGMF chairman writes that "the exemplary and mature leadership of General Superintendent Rudy Esperanza was well noted by the missionaries and Filipinos alike."[35] One downside of this trust, however, was that other leaders tended to put on Esperanza's shoulders tasks that were considered delicate or that nobody else wanted. This placed more responsibilities on one who already had his hands full.

General Council business sessions followed parliamentary procedures according to which each person had the right to speak up and be heard. In such a setting, debates and heated discussions often occurred. Esperanza was known for his tact in handling heated discussions during business sessions. Knowing that a Filipino might stand his ground or fight to the end just to save face, he would often call for a recess in the middle of a heated debate. While having snacks or during a meal, he would then approach the contending parties one at a time. He would joke with them to ease the tension. He would then hear them out and work out a solution or a compromise. This gave the contenders the opportunity to change their stand without losing face. Sometimes he would reconcile contending parties over lunch. When the session resumed, the contenders had already mellowed their stand and the issue was easily settled. At other times, he would say, "Let's table that," and then, "Next subject!" Tacitly, he would reprimand, and those concerned would stop their bickering. As recording secretary, Gallardo witnessed these proceedings and was impressed. Esperanza's charisma and winsome manner often cooled hot heads.[36]

There were also times when Esperanza's decisions or actions were questioned. In one General Council business session, two pastors brought up the rent being paid for the General Headquarters offices, claiming that the money spent was a "poor investment." Esperanza explained how the rental money was being raised, then acknowledged that he had failed God and accepted the situation as his fault.[37] No further explanation is given in the minutes, but what is striking is that Esperanza had no qualms about accepting his fault before all the pastors and missionaries gathered in that convention. Gallardo also recalls a meeting in which Esperanza was the object of a pastor's direct attack. Calmly, without taking offense, he responded, "We will look into that." Then during the recess, he went and talked to the pastor who had just questioned him.[38]

Esperanza did not avoid making difficult albeit firm decisions. The appointment of a pastor as National C. A. Secretary was questioned. After a long-drawn-out debate, Esperanza made an executive decision that the term of the C. A. Secretary would end that day, thus putting an end to the debate even if it could mean that he would bear the ire of the General Presbytery that had appointed the pastor to the post.[39]

There were those who accused Esperanza of taking sides. Some Filipino pastors accused him of siding with the Americans, while other Americans thought he was unjustly favoring the Filipinos. Observing all these, Gallardo concludes that if both Filipinos and American missionaries accused him of favoring the other side, then probably he was not taking any side but simply standing on his principles.[40] Esperanza avoided taking sides because, for him, missionaries and nationals must cooperate and unite efforts to effectively evangelize the Filipinos. He recognized that "[w]ith the rise of nationalism there may grow a tendency for spiritual independence availing not themselves of the knowledge, training, and experience of a foreign missionary. Any effort, therefore, that will promote the spiritual unity and united efforts of missionaries and nationals will be essential to fruitful service."[41]

Esperanza's approach to conflict resolution had its pros and cons. With the Filipino's value placed on respect for elders and those in positions of authority, contenders would often give in when approached by Esperanza in a congenial and paternal way. Respect for and loyalty to Esperanza often led contenders to agree to a compromise. Minutes of General Council proceedings and testimonies of individuals interviewed seldom record Esperanza directly confronting issues of conflict. He would either call for a recess, table the issue, or make a decision putting the weight of the matter on his own shoulders. Seemingly, unity was preserved. However, some deep issues were suppressed rather than resolved. Thus, when Esperanza was gone, they resurfaced. An example was the issue related to the control of Bethel Temple, which, like a violent and destructive volcanic eruption, led to a schism four years later.[42] Yet as long as Esperanza was the head, he was able to keep the denomination's united front intact.[43]

Esperanza's goal was a united PGCAG. Close associates and family members believe that the splintering of his beloved denomination as a result of the controversy over Bethel Temple could have broken his heart and contributed to his heart attack. Even a unifier like Esperanza would have been powerless to oppose the personal convictions and ambitions of people he had dearly loved.

Chapter 10

Far East Advanced School of Theology (now Asia Pacific Theological Seminary, Baguio City) first had classes on the BBI campus in Malinta, Valenzuela, Bulacan.
Source: Asia Pacific Research Center, APTS, Baguio City

CONCLUSIONS AND RECOMMENDATIONS

Conclusions

This research started with the hypothesis that "Rodrigo Esperanza's pioneering roles were foundational to the Assemblies of God in the Philippines and set the leadership pattern which helped propel the new denomination into rapid numerical growth." After establishing the PGCAG's rapid growth, I sought to present Esperanza's pioneering roles that laid the foundation of the PGCAG and aided the young denomination to grow quickly. To do so, I focused on the following five questions:

- What was Esperanza's formative background?
- What roles did he play in the history of the PGCAG?
- What factors influenced him in fulfilling his roles?
- What lasting impact did he have on the PGCAG?

- What benefits can the present PGCAG leaders receive from studying his leadership style?

I will now proceed to offer a concise answer to those questions. The benefits to present PGCAG leadership will be interwoven with the responses to the other questions.

Formative Background and Influences

Esperanza's parents were farmers in Pangasinan. He grew up working with his hands, accepting responsibilities in tending plants and animals. He was the eldest among the siblings and was endowed with intelligence, reaping academic honors from his elementary years onwards. The responsibilities given him as the eldest child, the full support of his family, and his intellectual abilities helped develop his self-confidence to face the rigors of life and gave him courage to leave the shelter of home and go to the USA. His self-confidence, his willingness to work, and his resilience helped him survive the Great Depression. These qualities also gave him determination when he returned to the Philippines to establish an Assemblies of God mission in the country.

Esperanza was born when the Philippines was under American rule. Thus, he was introduced to Protestantism at an early age. His education under American influence could have opened his mind to accept the teachings of Methodism. Propaganda about golden opportunities in America birthed in his heart the desire to seek his fortune in the US. There, instead of gold, he found God. His conversion gave him the desire to share the gospel with his own people. He started with Filipinos in the US, then returned to the Philippines to share the gospel message in his homeland. He studied in Bible school, doing summer jobs to support his schooling, contacted Filipino

Pentecostals ministering in the Philippines, got a license to preach from the USAG, organized the Filipino Pentecostal ministers in California, and then requested a USAG missionary to organize the AG work in the Philippines so as to give the group legal identity.

Foundational Roles in the PGCAG and Lasting Impact

Esperanza had a two-pronged purpose in returning to the Philippines in 1939: to share the Pentecostal gospel with his people, and to establish an Assemblies of God work in the country. He never lost sight of this purpose. The roles he played in the PGCAG can be understood better when seen in its light. Three of his foundational roles in the PGCAG were discussed in this book: organizer, evangelical leader, and district secretary/general superintendent.

Organizer

Esperanza's administrative and organizational skills were evident when he covered all bases in preparation for the organizational convention of the AG in the Philippines. He prepared himself by going to Bible school and getting a license to preach with the USAG. Before returning to the Philippines, he took a job in order to raise the needed finances. He also itinerated in the US to gain support for his mission. He helped organize the Filipino Pentecostal ministers in California, thereby increasing the network of possible support for the AG work back home. He also ensured the legality of the group by requesting a USAG missionary to head the work in the Philippines, thus fulfilling the requirements of the Philippine government.

When Esperanza returned to his hometown, he visited Filipino Pentecostal ministers who were not affiliated with any group and invited them to come to the AG's organizational convention. He wrote others whom he could not personally visit. In the organizational task, he joined forces with other Filipino Pentecostal ministers who shared the same desire to form an AG group in the country.

Those who attended the convention were mainly Ilocanos and some Visayans. They became the pioneer members when the Philippines District Council of the Assemblies of God was organized in March 1940. The PDCAG grew rapidly, with the exception of the war years. In 1953, the denomination became independent of the mother organization in the USA as the Philippines General Council of the Assemblies of God. Throughout the PDCAG/PGCAG's formative years, Esperanza played a crucial role as the first to hold the highest office available to a Filipino when the denomination was still a district of the USAG, and as the first General Superintendent when the denomination became independent.

Evangelical Leader

Even while studying in a Pentecostal Bible school in the US, Esperanza often attended services of other evangelical groups. His ecumenical mindset came to the fore when he sought to bring his denomination into fellowship with other Pentecostal and evangelical groups. He was undaunted by the fact that he had to face evangelicals' aversion to Pentecostals on the one hand, and some AG ministers' resistance to fellowship with "worldly Christians" on the other. It is interesting to note his intense loyalty to the AG and, at the same time, his openness to joining hands with other groups in evangelistic efforts such as a Billy Graham crusade.[1] Unfortunately, his efforts to bridge the gap between the AG and the rest of the evangelical community were cut short by his untimely death. However, his initial efforts opened doors of opportunity that later swung wide open for other AG leaders. This open-minded stance allowed the PGCAG to be in the center of the action when the Charismatic Renewal swept the country in the 1980s.

District Secretary/General Superintendent

Of the three roles discussed, the most important, with the greatest lasting impact, was Esperanza's role as the head of the PDCAG/PGCAG. Although an administrator, he was not one to stay long behind a desk. He was a hands-on leader, regularly visiting pastors and their churches, preaching, teaching, baptizing. Thus, he kept abreast of the needs and actual conditions of his constituents. He also kept constant communication with those he could not personally visit by diligently writing letters and reports and maintaining a regular column in the denomination's official magazine. As PGCAG head, his role was truly multifaceted. This book highlighted his other roles as evangelist, mentor, and visionary leader.

As an evangelist, he was ever conscious of the imminent return of Christ. Thus, he was a zealous evangelist himself as well as a zealous encourager for others to share the gospel since "night cometh when no one can work." This evangelistic zeal was an underlying motivation for many of his decisions and actions. He preached the gospel whenever and wherever the opportunity presented itself, whether in cities, towns, or the hinterlands. He fully supported the series of evangelistic and healing crusades sponsored by Lester Sumrall in Manila in the 1950s and 1960s. He also accompanied evangelists in their crusades in other major cities in the country. Indeed, Esperanza led the PGCAG in an evangelistic thrust which propelled the denomination into rapid growth and popularity.

Esperanza's mentoring model produced many ministers with the same zeal and passion for the ministry. Reading about his life reminded me so much of my own pastor in Iloilo Bethel Temple, Rev. Johnny Yasa, whom we called "Tatay"(Dad/Father) Yasa.

"Tatay Yasa" did not study at BBI, but he had mentors at IBI who were graduates of BBI, who in turn had been impacted by the life of Rudy Esperanza. I discovered that Esperanza and "Tatay Yasa" had the same evangelistic zeal, the same readiness and willingness to serve, the same self-sacrificing attitude, the same faith to accomplish things which are difficult or seemingly impossible. As I visited many other churches in the Visayas, northern Luzon, and Manila in my capacity as Bible college teacher and later as APRC archivist, I met many other "Tatay Yasas." While doing this research, I realized that they were actually many "Rudy Esperanzas." Esperanza's life showed those early pioneers how a pastor should minister, serve, live, and relate with others both in the church and outside the church. This model was passed on to other "Timothys."

Esperanza's visions were what surprised me most. When I joined the AG in 1974, there were few choices for Bible schools. In fact, when I enrolled at IBC in 1978, it was the only AG Bible school in the country that offered a bachelors degree. Presently the PGCAG has more than 30 Bible schools at various levels, from short-term institutes to CHED-accredited Bible colleges.[2] Back then, I knew of only one AG kindergarten school, the one run by BBI. Now there are church-based schools up to high school level. Moreover, the Filipino teachers in those schools are now receiving salaries covered by school fees. Back then, the PGCAG headquarters was still a dream. Now a three-story headquarters stands near the main gate of the BBC campus. Back then, there was a Sunday School Department. That has expanded and is now called the Education Department. Back then, the AG was buying Sunday School and Bible Study materials from the Philippine Association of Christian Education (PACE). Right now we are printing our own with the help of the ICI and APMM. APMM also publishes several Christian magazines and other Christian literature and has produced a series of Bible study videos and short movies with contemporary themes. The PGCAG headquarters has recently begun publishing a new official magazine, *Engage*. It is available in hard copy as well as PDF and JPEG versions downloadable from the PGCAG website. Radio programs continue to be aired. The General Council now has both Home Missions and World Missions departments. Other departments have also been created to meet the expanding needs of the denomination.

I once considered all the above projects to reflect the vision of the PGCAG's present leadership. I now realize that the seeds of these projects were planted by Esperanza. He lived to see the fruit of some of the seeds he had planted. For the other seeds, leaders who came after him cultivated his vision and brought forth fruit perhaps even beyond what Esperanza himself had envisioned. However, the present leaders have the same faith that dares to believe and fuels efforts to reach out for greater things in God's kingdom.

Yet over and above his various leadership roles, I firmly believe that what was most needed at that period of the PGCAG's life was Esperanza's ability to unite his denomination. His conflict resolution skills, his mentoring relationships, and his non-threatening humility gave him the capacity to maintain unity among Pentecostal ministers who all claimed the leading of the Holy Spirit, albeit in varied directions. His ability to defuse tense moments, personally talk to those of disagreeing camps, and come up with a compromise was proverbial. His constituents had witnessed that he was not self-serving but sought only the good of the body, nor did he care whether or not he received the honor for his service. Their trust in his character was translated into trust in his mediation efforts.

From 1940 to 1953, Esperanza was the top Filipino leader of the PDCAG under the USAG. From 1953 to 1969, he was the top

Filipino leader of the PGCAG as it transitioned to independence from more than a decade of dependence on the mother organization in the US. Throughout these years, he was striving to strike a balance among American missionaries who were not yet ready to yield control to nationals, nationals who were eager to gain control of the organization, nationals who still wanted to retain American leadership, and ministers who just wanted to be left alone to do their own work. On top of this, he had to deal with the ever-present regional biases among the national pastors. Despite all his efforts to deal fairly with the many issues brought before the General Council, he was accused by some of playing favorites. Keeping unity among a group of diverse worldviews was truly a difficult feat.

Two splits in the PGCAG occurred after Esperanza passed away. Currently, the denomination is again facing intense conflict at the national level. The PGCAG would do well to learn from Esperanza's approach to conflict resolution in order to keep the unity of the body intact.

Recommendations

This book is by no means comprehensive, limited as it is by the research questions. However, in the course of the study, other areas in the life of Esperanza have beckoned to the researcher, especially those related to current issues that ministers in general, and Pentecostal pastors in particular, are facing. For example, the research shows that although Esperanza sought to mentor his children, time spent with his wife was sacrificed. In view of this, I recommend that a study be made on his relationship with his wife, addressing questions like: How did Esperanza treat his wife? How did the Pentecostal worldview influence his relationship with her? In light of his frequent travels, how did he nurture his marriage? What conflicts between the couple were caused by his myriad duties and the expectations of his AG constituents? What kept their relationship intact despite the intense pressure placed upon them and their privacy? These are issues faced by Filipino ministerial couples, whether they be heading big organizations, pastoring small churches, or pioneering new ministries. In the various PGCAG ministerial fellowships I have attended, many Filipino pastors' wives have voiced their concerns about their relationships with their spouses. Even though research may show that Filipino ministerial couples' values and attitudes have changed over time, the principles remain the same. I believe Rudy and Leonor have much to teach the present generation of Filipino Pentecostal pastors and pastors' wives.

This research has focused on Esperanza's leadership roles. I recommend that another study be done of his leadership style, asking how it suited the worldview of both the Filipino AG constituents and the American AG missionaries of his time. Although multiplied scores of leadership studies have already been undertaken, the recommended study will focus on Esperanza as a Filipino Pentecostal leader. With Pentecostal groups mushrooming in the Philippines today, there is a growing need to address their leadership styles. Lessons learned from Esperanza's own leadership style could be extrapolated to determine what leadership style would best fit the worldview of the twenty-first-century Filipino Pentecostal constituents and foreign AG missionaries still ministering in the Philippines. Such a study could help to solve some of the various problems Filipino Pentecostal groups are facing.

To address the repeated splits in the denomination, I recommend to PGCAG leaders a two-pronged approach. The first approach is to take courses on conflict resolution and team building. Around 2006, my husband participated in planning the curriculum of an AGST program, the D.Min. in Peacemaking.

The need for such a program indicates the presence of discord in many churches in the country. Since more disputes are bound to arise, the PGCAG will benefit if its leaders learn basic principles in handling conflicts. It must be made clear, though, that the approach to conflict resolution needs to be culture-sensitive. Just as singing gospel songs in the local dialect make the message clearer to the people, using conflict resolution processes designed specifically for Filipinos would make the process more effective. One fact that all PGCAG leaders have to deal with is the varied cultural makeup of the denomination. This could be addressed using team building activities among the leaders of the various districts of the General Council. As previously stated, regional biases are prevalent in the country. Building appreciation for the strengths of each culture and striving to make cultural differences work for the benefit of the denomination would greatly counteract said biases. Appreciation and affirmation are great panacea for divisive tendencies.

The second approach is to seek the help of business and/or organizational consultants to study and evaluate the present structures of the PGCAG. I make this recommendation on the premise that the PGCAG's growth necessitates that it be run based on solid business policies and procedure. Furthermore, I have confidence that the current leadership has the needed theological foundation and spiritual insight to balance business procedures with biblical standards.

Once the above recommendation is taken, I recommend a subsequent course of action, i.e., to study the splits that plagued the denomination in the past. Using principles learned from conflict resolution courses, one can seek answers to questions like: What were the primary and secondary causes of the conflict? What led people to take sides in the conflict? What could have been done to avoid the split? What factors led to the reconciliation in 1979? What principles could be applied to the conflicts the PGCAG has repeatedly faced and is, in fact, facing right now? What proactive steps could be done to avoid splits in the future?

In the introduction, I mentioned two other factors that stood out as keys to the growth of the PGCAG: Bible schools and denominational publications. I now include those two factors in my recommendations.

I recommend that studies be made of the influence exerted by the *Bulletin*, the *Pentecostal Voice*, and other early magazines on the development of the PGCAG's theology and ethos. The influence of these magazines was touched on briefly in this paper. A study of these publications will give insight into the development of the PGCAG's theology that exerted such a strong influence on the denomination's culture and philosophy. This insight will help leaders to better understand issues that persist up to the present. Moreover, changes in the denomination's philosophy and character can be clarified by studying more recent denominational publications. John Carter, APTS president for many years, often said, "Policies have history."[3] In the same way, theology has history. Understanding the development of theology will help in understanding choices that people make and actions that they take. This is crucial in the ministry.

I also recommend that studies be made of the influence exerted by regional Bible schools on the kind of ministers leading the denomination. It is common knowledge that character and values are more caught than taught. Esperanza dedicated much of his time and effort to mentoring Bible school students, knowing that they were the future leaders of the denomination. Studies could show whether intentional mentoring is happening in the Bible schools and, if so, what character and values are being passed on. Bible school faculty recognize that every student they teach will teach many more, whether for good or bad. Such a grave responsibility necessitates intentional study.

Finally, in all the PGCAG churches, I recommend that, as much as possible, a basic course on Church History concluding with an account of the beginnings of the PGCAG be offered. The great Alexander Solzhenitsyn once said, "There is an aphorism: He who forgets his own history is condemned to repeat it. If we don't know our own history, we will simply have to endure all the same mistakes, sacrifices, and absurdities all over again." Sadly, this is the experience of the Assemblies of God in the Philippines. Philip Schaff likewise wrote, "How shall we labor with any effect to build up the church, if we have no thorough knowledge of her history, or fail to apprehend it from the proper point of observation? History is, and must ever continue to be, next to God's Word, the richest foundation of wisdom, and the surest guide to all successful practical activity."[4] Moreover, a Filipino adage says, *"Ang hindi marunong lumingon sa pinanggalingan ay hindi makararating sa parororoonan."* (He who does not look back to where he came from cannot arrive at where he is going.) All these sayings point to the importance of studying our history. Sadly, not many see the significance of this. Dr. Ronaldo Mactal, former chair of the History Department of De La Salle University, Taft, and my Historiography Professor, told the class that, in the Philippines, historians are a rare breed. In another conversation, Dr. Azriel Azarcon's rejoinder to this comment was, "Church historians are an endangered species." It is my hope that as church members begin to study Church History and come to realize its importance, more people will appreciate their Christian heritage and catch the vision of imparting to the present generation wisdom learned from the Church's past.

ENDNOTES

Pastors Ruben and David Candelaria flanking Evangelist Oral Roberts to his left and right respectively. Taken at the Quirino Grandstand, Luneta, after the evangelistic service in 1964. Rev. Esperanza is second from right behind Pastor David.
Source: Esperanza Collection, Asia Pacific Research Center, APTS, Baguio City

Chapter 1

[1] Trinidad C. Esperanza, "The Assemblies of God in the Philippines" (MRE thesis, Fuller Theological Seminary, 1965), 15.

[2] Arthur Tuggy, *The Philippine Church: Growth in a Changing Society*, Church Growth Series (Grand Rapids, MI: William B. Eerdmans, 1971), 151-2.

[3] Wonsuk Ma, "Philippines," in *The New International Dictionary of Pentecostal and Charismatic Movements*, Revised Edition, Stanley Burgess (Grand Rapids, MI: Zondervan, 2002), 201.

[4] John W. Kennedy, "The Philippines: Embracing the Challenge," *Pentecostal Evangel*, 4 June 2000, 5. (A PGCAG official informed me that the denomination, as of mid-2010, already had 4,000 churches. However, no definite record was available at the time of the conversation.)

[5] "Largest Denominations: Philippines," *DAWN Philippines: A Report on the State of the Evangelical Churches in the Philippines 2000*, with a foreword by Bishop Efraim M. Tendero (n.p. and n.d.), 40.

[6] Ma, 201.

[7] Kenton J. Clymer, *Protestant Missionaries in the Philippines, 1898-1916: An Inquiry into the American Colonial Mentality* (Chicago: University of Illinois Press, 1986), 34.

[8] Reuben Arthur Torrey, *Is the Present Tongues Movement of God?* (LA: Biola Book Room, n.d.), 4; quoted in Edith L. Blumhofer, *Restoring the Faith: The Assemblies of God, Pentecostalism, and American Culture* (Chicago: University of Illinois Press, 1993), 106-7.

[9] E.g., Mamerto Garsulao, interview by author, 18 April 2002, Iloilo City, Philippines, transcript, PGCAG Oral History Collection, Asia Pacific Research Center, Asia Pacific Theological Seminary, Baguio City, Philippines, 26; Roque Sr. and Estrella Cagas Interview, interview by author, 11 April 2002, Talisay, Cebu, Philippines, transcript, PGCAG Oral History Collection, Asia Pacific Research Center, Asia Pacific Theological Seminary, Baguio City, Philippines, 19; Rosendo and Presentacion Alcantara First Interview, interview by author, 4 July 2001, Bakersfield, CA, transcript, APRC Oral History Collection, Asia Pacific Research Center, Asia Pacific Theological Seminary, Baguio City, Philippines, 10; Marcelo Arangote, interview by author, 23 April 2003, BBC Campus, Malinta, Valenzuela, MM, Philippines, transcript, APRC Oral History Collection, Asia Pacific Research Center, Asia Pacific Theological Seminary, Baguio City, Philippines, 12.

¹⁰Anacleto Lobarbio, interview by author, 20 January 2006, transcript, APRC Oral History Collection, Asia Pacific Research Center, Asia Pacific Theological Seminary, Baguio City, Philippines, 3-11 *passim.*
¹¹James H. Montgomery and Donald A. McGavran, *The Discipling of a Whole Nation* (Milpitas, CA: Global Church Growth, 1980), 132.
¹²E.g., Pedro S. de Achutegui and Miguel A. Bernad, *Religious Revolution in the Philippines: The Life and Church of Gregorio Aglipay* (Manila, Philippines: Ateneo de Manila, 1966); Nestor Bunda, *A Mission History of the Philippine Baptist Churches 1898-1998 from a Philippine Perspective* (Aachen, Germany: Verlag an der Lottbek im Besitz des Verlags Mainz, 1999); T. Valentino Sitoy Jr. *Several Springs, One Stream: The United Church of Christ in the Philippines,* vol. 1, *Heritage and Origins (1898-1948)* (Quezon City, Philippines: United Church of Christ in the Philippines, 1992); and Ruben F. Trinidad, *A Monument to Religious Nationalism: History and Polity of the IEMELIF Church* (Quezon City: Evangelical Methodist Church in the Philippines, 1999).
¹³Melba P. Maggay, *The Gospel in Filipino Context* (Mandaluyong City, Philippines: OMF Literature, 1987), 33.

Chapter 2

¹Allan Anderson, *An Introduction to Pentecostalism* (Cambridge: Cambridge University Press, 2004), 38.¹
²William K. Kay, *Pentecostalism* (London: SCM Press, 2009), xvii.
³Edith L. Blumhofer, *Restoring the Faith: The Assemblies of God, Pentecostalism, and American Culture* (Chicago: University of Illinois Press, 1993), 47; A. Anderson, 34.
⁴Blumhofer, *Restoring the Faith,* 50.
⁵Kay, 52. See also A. Anderson, 33-4.
⁶Blumhofer, *Restoring the Faith,* 50.
⁷James R. Goff Jr., "Parham, Charles Fox," in *NIDPCM,* 956.
⁸A. Anderson, 34.
⁹Blumhofer, *Restoring the Faith,* 52.
¹⁰Goff, "Parham, Charles Fox," 956.
¹¹Cecil M. Robeck Jr., "Farrow, Lucy F.," in *NIDPCM,* 632. Cox states that Farrow was once Parham's governess. Harvey Cox, *Fire from Heaven: The Rise of Pentecostal Spirituality and the Reshaping of Religion in the Twenty-first Century* (Reading, MA: Addison-Wesley, 1995), 49.
¹²Cox, 49-50.
¹³Ibid., 50.
¹⁴Cecil M. Robeck Jr., "Seymour, William Joseph," in *NIDPCM,* 1055.
¹⁵Ibid.
¹⁶Cecil M. Robeck Jr., "Azusa Street Revival," in *NIDPCM,* 345.
¹⁷Ibid. Brumback records that Seymour received the baptism and spoke in tongues on April 12, 1906. Carl Brumback, *Suddenly . . . From Heaven: A History of the Assemblies of God* (Springfield, MO: Gospel Publishing House, 1961), 36.
¹⁸Cecil M. Robeck Jr., *The Azusa Street Mission and Revival: The Birth of the Global Pentecostal Movement* (Nashville, TN: Thomas Nelson, 2006), 6-7.
¹⁹G. Raymond Carlson, D. V. Hurst, and Cyril E. Homer, *The Assemblies of God in Mission* (Springfield, MO: Gospel Publishing House, 1970), 7.
²⁰Gary B. McGee, *This Gospel Shall be Preached.* Vol. 1: *A History and Theology of Assemblies of God Foreign Missions to 1959* (Springfield, MO: Gospel Publishing House, 1986), 1:74.
²¹William W. Menzies, *Anointed to Serve: The Story of the Assemblies of God, Vol. 1* (Springfield, MO: Gospel Publishing House, 1971), 81.
²²Walter J. Hollenweger, *The Pentecostals,* trans. R. A. Wilson (London: SCM, 1972), 29.

[23]Klaude Kendrick, *The Promise Fulfilled: A History of the Modern Pentecostal Movement* (Springfield, MO: Gospel Publishing House, 1961), 71.
[24]Blumhofer, *Restoring the Faith*, 116.
[25]Menzies, 80-84.
[26]Ethel E. Goss, *The Winds of God* (NY: Comet Press, 1958), 163; quoted in Menzies, 82.
[27]E. N. Bell, ed., "General Convention of Pentecostal Saints and Churches of God in Christ," *Word and Witness*, 20 December 1913, 1, Flower Pentecostal Heritage Center CD Collection, Asia Pacific Research Center, Asia Pacific Theological Seminary, Baguio City, Philippines
[28]Ibid.
[29]Blumhofer, *Restoring the Faith*, 124.
[30]Menzies, 97. Blumhofer says the attendees represented "seventeen states and missions in Egypt and South Africa." Blumhofer, *Restoring the Faith*, 116.
[31]Kendrick, 84.
[32]E. N. Bell, ed., "Hot Springs Assembly; God's Glory Present," *Word and Witness*, 20 April 1914, 1, Flower Pentecostal Heritage Center CD Collection, Asia Pacific Research Center, Asia Pacific Theological Seminary, Baguio City, Philippines.
[33]"Constitution and By-Laws of the General Council of the Assemblies of God Including Essential Resolutions Revised and Adopted, September 16-22, 1927," 3-4, Flower Pentecostal Heritage Center CD Collection, Asia Pacific Research Center, Asia Pacific Theological Seminary, Baguio City, Philippines.
[34]Irwin Winehouse, *The Assemblies of God: A Popular Survey* (New York: Vantage Press, 1959), 31.
[35]E. N. Bell and J. R. Flower, "In Doctrines," *The Christian Evangel*, 1 August 1914, 2; quoted in Blumhofer, *The Assemblies of God*, 1:209.
[36]Blumhofer, *Restoring the Faith*, 124.
[37]Ibid., 125.
[38]Ibid., 126-27.
[39]Menzies, 111.
[40]Ibid.
[41]Robert Mapes Anderson, *Vision of the Disinherited: The Making of American Pentecostalism* (Oxford: Oxford University Press, 1979), 177.
[42]Ibid., 177-78.
[43]Gregory A. Boyd, *Oneness Pentecostals and the Trinity* (Grand Rapids, MI: Baker, 1992), 139-40; emphasis in the original.
[44]Brumback, 201-2.
[45]Kay, 79.
[46]Brumback, 210. Blumhofer states that this was more than twenty-five percent of the ministerial roll. Blumhofer, *Restoring the Faith*, 134.
[47]R. Anderson, 183.
[48]Blumhofer, *Restoring the Faith*, 135.
[49]Ibid., 32. Blumhofer gives his full name as Fred Francis Bosworth. Blumhofer, *Restoring the Faith*, 135.
[50]Menzies, 127.
[51]Brumback, 217.
[52]Blumhofer, *Restoring the Faith*, 136.
[53]Menzies, 129-30.
[54]Blumhofer, *Restoring the Faith*, 4.
[55]Brumback, Appendix D, "Current Statistics: Assemblies of God Ordained Ministers," 365.
[56]Brumback, Appendix D, "Current Statistics: Assemblies of God Churches," 367.
[57]Brumback, Appendix D, "Current Statistics: Assemblies of God Membership," 366. Brumback states that 1925 was the first year with complete records.

58"A Missionary Movement," *Pentecostal Evangel*, 13 November 1920, 8, Flower Pentecostal Heritage Center CD Collection, Asia Pacific Research Center, Asia Pacific Theological Seminary, Baguio City, Philippines.

59"Minutes of the Seventh General Council, 1919," 12, Flower Pentecostal Heritage Center CD Collection, Asia Pacific Research Center, Asia Pacific Theological Seminary, Baguio City, Philippines.

60Noel Perkin, "Qualifications for Missionary Service," Noel Perkin File, Assemblies of God Archives, Springfield, MO, n.d.; quoted in Edith L. Blumhofer, *Pentecost in My Soul: Explorations in the Meaning of Pentecostal Experience in the Early Assemblies of God* (Springfield, MO: Gospel Publishing House, 1989), 150.

61Brumback, Appendix E, "Foreign Missions Survey: Assemblies of God Missionaries," 368.

62Ibid, 370.
63Ibid, 369.
64Ibid.
65Ibid.

Chapter 3

[1] Dionisio S. Salazar and Lourdes C. Ungson, *Philippine Development and Progress* (Quezon City, Philippines: Taurus, 1974), 44-45.

[2] Nestor Distor Bunda, *A Mission History of the Philippine Baptist Churches 1898-1998 from a Philippine Perspective* (Aachen, Germany: Verlag an der Lottbek im Besitz des Verlags Mainz, 1999), 59.

[3] Gerald H. Anderson, "Providence and Politics behind Protestant Missionary Beginnings in the Philippines," in *Studies in Philippine Church History*, ed. Gerald H. Anderson (London: Cornell University Press, 1969), 294.

[4] Teodoro A. Agoncillo, *History of the Filipino People*, 8th ed. (Quezon City, Philippines: Garotech Publishing, 1999), 231.

[5] Rudyard Kipling, "The White Man's Burden," first stanza, available at http://www.online-literature.com/keats/922/, accessed February 11, 2012.

[6] G. Anderson, 293.

[7] Antonio M. Molina, *The Philippines through the Centuries*, vol. 2 (Manila, Philippines: Antonio M. Molina, 1961), 2:243.

[8] Sharon Delmendo, *The Star-Entangled Banner* (Quezon City, Philippines: University of the Philippines Press, 2005), 11.

[9] Molina, 2:244.

[10] Renato Constantino, *The Philippines: A Past Revisited* (Quezon City, Philippines: Renato Constantino, 1975), 314.

[11] Molina, 2:244.
[12] Salazar and Ungson, 313.
[13] Ibid., 314.
[14] Ibid., 311-12.
[15] Constantino, 369.

[16] F. Landa Jocano, "Filipino Social Structure and Value System," in *Filipino Cultural Heritage*, ed. F. Landa Jocano, Filipino Social Structure and Value Orientation, no. 2 (Manila, Philippines: Philippine Women's University, 1966), 15.

[17] Melba P. Maggay, *The Gospel in Filipino Context* (Mandaluyong City, Philippines: OMF Literature, 1987), 4.

[18] Leonardo N. Mercado, *Elements of Filipino Philosophy*, rev. ed., in *Doing Filipino Theology*, Asia Pacific Missiological Series, no. 6, ed. Leonardo N. Mercado (Manila, Philippines: Divine Word Publications, 1997), 162.

[19] Michael L. Tan, *Usug, Kulam, Pasma: Traditional Concepts of Health and Illness in the Philippines*, Traditional Medicine in the Philippines: Research Reports, no. 3, eds.

Lorna P. Makil and Mary Grenough (Quezon City, Philippines: Alay Kapwa Kilusang Pangkalusugan, 1987), 81; emphasis in original.

[20] Maggay, 24.

[21] Jaime Bulatao, "The 'Hiya' System in Filipino Culture," in *Filipino Cultural Heritage*, ed. Jocano, 32.

[22] Mercado, 171.

[23] Domingo J. Diel Jr., "Perspectives on Baptist Church History," in *Chapters in Philippine Church History*, ed. Anne C. Kwantes (Manila, Philippines: OMF Literature, 2001), 226.

[24] G. Anderson, 280-1.

[25] Mariano C. Apilado, *Revolutionary Spirituality: A Study of the Protestant Role in the American Colonial Rule of the Philippines, 1898-1928* (Quezon City, Philippines: New Day, 1999), 52.

[26] T. Valentino Sitoy, Jr., *Several Springs, One Stream: The United Church of Christ in the Philippines*, vol. 1, *Heritage and Origins (1898-1948)* (Quezon City: United Church of Christ in the Philippines, 1992), 27-68. Anne Kwantes gives the date of the arrival of James B. Rodgers in Manila to be April 21, 1899. Anne C. Kwantes, "Presbyterian Missionaries in the Philippines: A Historical Analysis of their Contributions to Social Change (1899-1910)" (Ph.D. diss., University of the Philippines, 1988), iv.

[27] Board of Managers of American Baptist Foreign Mission Society and Woman's American Baptist Foreign Mission Society, 1925, 7; quoted in Bunda, 93.

[28] Kenton J. Clymer, *Protestant Missionaries in the Philippines, 1898-1916: An Inquiry into the American Colonial Mentality* (Chicago: University of Illinois Press, 1986), 14-15.

[29] Kwantes, 297-299.

[30] Ibid., 253.

[31] Agoncillo, 371.

[32] Donald McGavran, *Multiplying Churches in the Philippines* (Manila: United Church of Christ in the Philippines, 1958), 5.

[33] Kenton J. Clymer, "Protestant Missionaries and American Colonialism in the Philippines, 1899-1916: Attitudes, Perceptions, Involvement," in *Reappraising an Empire: New Perspectives on Philippine American History*, ed. Peter W. Stanley (Cambridge, MA: Harvard University Press, 1984), 158.

[34] Clymer, *Protestant Missionaries in the Philippines*, 95-97.

[35] See Frank Charles Laubach, *The People of the Philippines: Their Religious Progress and Preparation for Spiritual Leadership in the Far East* (New York: George H. Duran, 1925), ch. 16: "Filipino Laymen Who Have Met the Test," 272-89.

[36] Averell U. Aragon, "The Philippine Council of Evangelical Churches," in *Chapters in Philippine Church History*, ed. Anne C. Kwantes (Manila, Philippines: OMF Literature, 2001), 383.

[37] Agoncillo, 373.

[38] Andrew F. Walls, *The Missionary Movement in Christian History: Studies in the Transmission of Faith* (Maryknoll, NY: Orbis, 1996), 212.

[39] Nick Joaquin, *Culture and History* (Mandaluyong City, Philippines: Anvil Publishing, 2004), 326.

[40] Ibid., 327

[41] Clymer, "Protestant Missionaries and American Colonialism in the Philippines," 159.

[42] [Horace McCracken], *History of Church of God Missions* (Cleveland, TN: Church of God Publishing House, 1943), 19.

[43] Charles W. Conn, *Where the Saints Have Trod: A History of Church of God Missions* (Cleveland, TN: Pathway Press, 1959), 228-9.

[44] Ibid., 229.

⁴⁵Oscar S. Suarez, *Protestantism and Authoritarian Politics* (Quezon City, Philippines: New Day, 1999), 20.

⁴⁶Lamin Sanneh, *Translating the Message: The Missionary Impact on Culture*, American Society of Missiology Series, no. 13 (Maryknoll, NY: Orbis, 1989), 90.

⁴⁷Ibid., 106.

⁴⁸Ibid., 208.

⁴⁹Clymer, *Protestant Missionaries in the Philippines*, 16-17.

⁵⁰Peter G. Gowing, *Islands Under the Cross: The Story of the Church in the Philippines* (Manila, Philippines: National Council of Churches in the Philippines, 1967), 186.

⁵¹Ma, 201.

⁵²Benjamin H. Caudle, "Application for Appointment as Missionary by the Foreign Missions Department, General Council of the Assemblies of God, April 28, 1924," USAG Missionary Pioneers, Dave Johnson Archives, Asia Pacific Research Center, Asia Pacific Theological Seminary, Baguio City, Philippines, 1; "Assemblies of God Beginnings," *Focus-Philippines*, USAG Missionary Pioneers, Dave Johnson Archives, Asia Pacific Research Center, Asia Pacific Theological Seminary, Baguio City, 10. Dave Johnson, *Led by the Spirit: The History of the American Assemblies of God Missionaries in the Philippines* (Pasig City, Philippines: ICI Ministries, 2009), 7.

⁵³B. H. Caudle, "Opportunities in Manila, 8.27.27," and "Manila, Philippine Islands, 3.10.28," USAG Missionary Pioneers, Dave Johnson Archives, Asia Pacific Research Center, Asia Pacific Theological Seminary, Baguio City, 5.

⁵⁴Noel Perkin, "Coordination and Advance (1925-1930)," *The Pentecostal Evangel* (December 27, 1964) and a letter from B. H. Caudle to Noel Perkin, January 12, 1965; quoted in Trinidad E. Seleky, "Six Filipinos and One American: Pioneers of the Assemblies of God in the Philippines," *Asian Journal of Pentecostal Studies* 4, no. 1 (2001): 121. The year the Caudles left the Philippines is not clear. However, the "Missionaries by Country" list obtained from the USAG Department of Foreign Missions archives in 2001 gives "12-31-1930" as the year of service of the Caudles in the Philippines. Since it is established that the couple arrived in the Philippines in 1926, it is possible that they left the country in 1930. "Missionaries by Country," Flower Pentecostal Heritage Center, USAG Headquarters, Springfield, MO, 2.

⁵⁵Crispulo Garsulao took the name "Cris Garsulas" when he went to the States because "lao" sounded Chinese and he was often grouped with the Chinese. Garsulao interview, 2.

⁵⁶Ibid., 29.

⁵⁷T. Esperanza, 19.

⁵⁸"Another Graduate Left for the Foreign Field," *Glad Tidings*, February 1928, 9.

⁵⁹"In the Service of the King: Sibalem [sic], Antique, P.I.," *Glad Tidings*, May 1928, 8. The record here shows that he visited "B. M. Claude," an obvious misspelling of Caudle's last name.

⁶⁰Ibid.

⁶¹At first the church was simply identified as "Pentecostal" but later named Villar Assembly of God Church. It is thus considered the first Assemblies of God church founded on Filipino soil. It was not named Assembly of God at the start because the denomination was not established in the Philippines until 1940. Information given by Mamerto Garsulao on a card dated December 12, 2002, sent to the author.

⁶²"Sebalom [sic], Antique, P. I.," *Glad Tidings*, November 1930, 10.

⁶³"In the Service of the King," *Glad Tidings*, June 1933, 8.

⁶⁴"Antique, P.I.," *Glad Tidings*, March 1934, 12.

⁶⁵Garsulao interview, 25.

⁶⁶"Promoted to Glory," *Glad Tidings*, March 1935, news clipping, Department of Foreign Missions Archives, USAG Headquarters, Springfield, MO, 2-1.

[67]"Brief Historical Perspective of the Philippine General Council of the Assemblies of God," *Intercom*, June 1994, 1. The account above does not include Emil Bernaldez, a graduate of Central Bible College, who left the US in 1929 to pioneer work among his people in Bohol. "[No title], November 30, 1929," news clipping, Department of Foreign Missions Archives, USAG Headquarters, Springfield, MO, 2-7.

[68]Ibid.

[69]Rudy C. Esperanza, "The Need in the Philippine Islands," *The Missionary Challenge*, July 1948, 15.

[70]R. Esperanza, "Why I Am a Minister of the Assembly of God," 2-3.

[71]Ibid., 3.

[72]PDCAG, "Minutes of the First Annual Meeting of the Philippines District Council of the Assemblies of God, Inc." (Valenzuela City, Bulacan, Philippines: PGCAG Headquarters Archives, 1940), 1.

[73]Ibid., 2.

[74]Ibid., 5-6.

[75]Ibid., 4.

[76]R. Esperanza, "The Need in the Philippine Islands," 15.

[77]Agoncillo, 387.

[78]Ibid., 410.

[79]Rosendo and Presentacion Alcantara, 2nd Interview, interview by author, 7 July 2001, Bakersfield, CA, transcript, APRC Oral History Collection, Asia Pacific Research Center, Asia Pacific Theological Seminary, Baguio City, Philippines, 5-8.

[80]Noel Perkin, Appointment Certification, 22 February 1946 (Valenzuela City, Philippines: PGCAG Headquarters Archives, 1967).

[81]Rodrigo Esperanza Affidavit, 14 August 1946 (Valenzuela City, Philippines: PGCAG Headquarters Archives, 1967).

[82]Ma, 201.

[83]PGCAG, "Minutes of the Philippines General Council of the Assemblies of God 1st Annual Convention" (Valenzuela City, Bulacan, Philippines: PGCAG Headquarters Archives, 1953), 2-3.

[84]Eleazer E. Javier, "The Pentecostal Legacy," in *Supplement to Chapters in Philippine Church History*, ed. Anne C. Kwantes (Manila, Philippines: OMF Literature, 2002), 71.

[85]Ibid., 73.

[86]Unless otherwise stated, the information in this paragraph was taken from Eleazer Javier, "A Brief History of the Messiah Community Church (Formerly the Taytay Methodist Community Church)," January 2007, 3-6.

[87]The Taytay Methodist Church's active support of the AG healing revivals bolstered the image of the AG in Manila during those early years when it was not yet known in the Tagalog area. Luther Jeremiah Oconer, "The *Culto Pentecostal* Story: Holiness Revivalism and the Making of Philippine Methodist Identity, 1899-1965" (Ph.D. diss., Drew University, 2009), 183.

[88]Eleazer Javier, "Our Pentecostal Legacy," lecture, 15 September 2001, ICS, Mandaluyong, APRC Oral History Collection, Asia Pacific Research Center, Asia Pacific Theological Seminary, Baguio City, Philippines, 4.

[89]Blumhofer defines "classical Pentecostals" as "[North] American Pentecostals who trace their heritage from 1901." Blumhofer, *Restoring the Faith*, 2; see also A. Anderson, 10.

[90]Luther Oconer, "The Manila Healing Revival and the First Pentecostal Defections in the Methodist Church in the Philippines," *Pneuma* 31 (2009): 79. Note: Other "Javiers" will be mentioned in this paper, but from this point on, "Javier" will be used to refer to Eleazer Javier.

[91]Oconer, "The *Culto Pentecostal* Story," 192.

[92]Lobarbio interview, 20 January 2006, *passim* 3-11.

[93] Montgomery and McGavran, 115.
[94] E. Javier, "The Pentecostal Legacy," 75.
[95] Ma, 201-2.
[96] E. Javier, "The Pentecostal Legacy," 82.
[97] *SOS Manual* (Philippines: FARM, 2012), 7.
[98] The author was in a PGCAG leadership meeting in July 2012 in Cebu City when the PGCAG General Secretary explained his office's project to update PGCAG statistical data.

Chapter 4

[1] Dionisio Esperanza, "R. C. Esperanza: Early life events as told by his father," n.d., n.p. This account of Rudy's life from birth till his departure for the US was handwritten on three sheets of bond paper placed inside an official envelope of the Northern Luzon District Council of the Assemblies of God in the Philippines. The label on the envelope is now used as title of this record. The author was obviously someone who had interviewed Rudy's father. However, the interviewer did not indicate his/her name on the papers. This interview record was part of Rodrigo Esperanza's documents turned over to me when I accepted the responsibility of setting up the APTS archives. The record is presently kept in the Rodrigo Esperanza Collection of the Asia Pacific Research Center, Asia Pacific Theological Seminary, Baguio City, Philippines.

[2] Jesse Bautista, interview by author, 24 March 2011, Pozorrubio, Pangasinan, Philippines, handwritten notes in the hand of author, Rodrigo Esperanza Documentary Project.

[3] Names of Rudy's living family members at the time of his death were listed on a typewritten Obituary text presently kept in the Rodrigo Esperanza Collection of the Asia Pacific Research Center, Asia Pacific Theological Seminary, Baguio City, Philippines.

[4] There were few hospitals in the country in the early 1900s, so most Filipino babies were born in their homes. Since Rudy's parents lived in a barrio, his mother obviously gave birth at home with the aid of a *comadrona*, a local midwife.

[5] Unless otherwise stated, information in this section is based on Dionisio Esperanza's interview record.

[6] R. Esperanza, "Why I Am a Minister of the Assembly of God," 1.

[7] T. Esperanza, 18.

[8] R. Esperanza, "Why I Am a Minister of the Assembly of God," 1.

[9] D. Esperanza, 3.

[10] Unless otherwise indicated, material in this section on Rodrigo Esperanza's salvation and call to the ministry comes from his own manuscript, "Why I Am a Minister of the Assembly of God."

[11] Anacleto Lobarbio, interview by author, 16 February 2011, Pasig City, Metro Manila, Philippines, transcript in the hand of author, Rodrigo Esperanza Documentary Project, 1.

[12] Oconer attests that Esperanza was a former exhorter of the Methodist Episcopal Church. Oconer, "The *Culto Pentecostal* Story," 174.

[13] Rosario First Assembly of God Church. "Tribute to the Church Pioneer Pastor," typewritten manuscript, 1969, 1.

[14] Jesse Bautista, interview by author, 24 March 2011, Pozorrubio, Pangasinan, Philippines, transcript in the hand of author, Rodrigo Esperanza Documentary Project, 2.

[15] Daniel Esperanza, handwritten list of positions held by R. C. Esperanza, n.d., 3.

[16] One cannot help but wonder how a once-Methodist licensed Exhorter could doubt his salvation. One can only surmise that his understanding of the Methodist teaching on entire sanctification could have denied him the assurance of his salvation when he drifted from the faith. In the same vein, the Wesleyan openness to "rich and vivid religious experience" could have made Esperanza receptive to the Pentecostal experience,

accepting the "finished work" message so that he could finally testify that he was "born again."

[17][Rodrigo Esperanza], Diary 1937-1939, Rodrigo Esperanza Collection, Asia Pacific Research Center, Asia Pacific Theological Seminary, Baguio City, Philippines, April 13, 1939 entry.

[18]There are a number of cases where Esperanza has been quoted directly. To communicate his authenticity, the publisher's editing team has opted to leave the original grammar in place in most cases.

Chapter 5

[1]Unless otherwise stated, information in this section is taken from Esperanza, "Why I Am a Minister of the Assembly of God."

[2]"The International Assemblies of the First Born," available at http://www.iafb.us/history.html, accessed December 4, 2012.

[3]For example, he visited Ptr. Abrenica in Villasis on June 15, 1939, Ptr. Mariano Gonzales in San Nicolas on June 20, and Ptr. Alcantara in Dingras on June 22. R. Esperanza, Diary 1937-1939.

[4]R. Esperanza, "Why I Am a Minister of the Assembly of God," 3.

[5]PDCAG, "Minutes of the First Annual Meeting," 1.

[6]Ibid., 6.

[7]Rudy C. Esperanza, "District Superintendent's Annual Report," *Bulletin*, May 1950, 16.

[8]Ibid., 16. Mariano Gonzales, interview by author, 8 May 2003, San Nicolas, Ilocos Norte, Philippines, transcript, PGCAG Oral History Collection, Asia Pacific Research Center, Asia Pacific Theological Seminary, Baguio City, Philippines, 6.

[9]E.g., see R. C. Esperanza, Diary 1937-1939, Rodrigo Esperanza Collection, Asia Pacific Research Center Archives, Asia Pacific Theological Seminary, Baguio City, Philippines, Jan. 26, Feb. 13, and Nov. 28, 1939 entries.

[10]Rudy C. Esperanza, "The Church: Its Organizational Structure, Its Relevance to This Hour," *Pentecostal Voice*, July 1969, 5.

[11]Rudy C. Esperanza, "Superintendent's Report," *Bulletin*, November-December 1949, 10.

[12]Rudy C. Esperanza, "District Superintendent's Report," *Bulletin*, February 1950, 8.

[13]Rudy C. Esperanza, "District Superintendent's Annual Report," *Bulletin*, April 1951, 13.

[14]Rudy C. Esperanza, "Superintendent's Report." *Bulletin*, May 1952, 5-6.

[15]Alcantara first interview, 5.

[16]R. Esperanza, "The Church," 5.

[17]R. Esperanza, "Annual Report," April 1951, 13. R. C. Esperanza, "The District Council: God is Doing a New Thing in the Philippines," *Bulletin*, October 1950, 3; emphasis mine.

[18]Arangote interview, 6.

[19]Eleazer E. Javier, interview by author, 17 February 2011, Taytay, Rizal, Philippines, transcript in hand of author, Rodrigo Esperanza Documentary Project, 5.

[20]Aragona interview, 6.

[21]Narciso Colcolen, interview by author, 15 April 2003, Bussot, Gregorio del Pilar, Ilocos Sur, Philippines, transcript, APRC Oral History Collection, Asia Pacific Research Center, Asia Pacific Theological Seminary, Baguio City, Philippines, 14. "'*Bayanihan*' literally means, 'being a *bayan*,' and is thus used to refer to a spirit of communal unity and cooperation." "*Bayanihan,*" available at http://groups.csail.mit.edu/cag/bayanihan/bayanword.html, accessed December 15, 2012.

[22]Arangote interview, 16.

[23]Garsulao interview, 20.

²⁴R. Esperanza, "The Church," 5.
²⁵E. Javier interview, 17 February 2011, 5.
²⁶Oconer, "The Manila Healing Revival," 67.
²⁷Lester Sumrall, *The True Story of Clarita Villanueva* (Manila, Philippines: by the author, 1955), 109-10.
²⁸Carmelita A. Gallardo, interview by author, 18 February 2011, Southern Tagalog District Council Office, Bethel Bible College Campus, Malinta, Valenzuela, MM, Philippines, transcript in the hand of author, Rodrigo Esperanza Documentary Project, 10-12.
²⁹Eleazer Javier, interview by author, 17 February 2011, Taytay, Metro Manila, Philippines, transcript in the hand of author, Rodrigo Esperanza Documentary Project, 5; Anacleto Lobarbio, pre-video interview, interview by author, 16 February 2011, Pasig City, MM, Philippines, transcript in the hand of author, Rodrigo Esperanza Documentary Project, 8.
³⁰R. Esperanza, "The Church," 5.
³¹E. Javier, "Our Pentecostal Legacy."

Chapter 6

¹See "Background and Birth of the PGCAG," p. 47.
²Perkin, Appointment Certification.
³R. Esperanza, Affidavit, 2.
⁴Leland Johnson, comment handwritten on p. 3 of R. Esperanza, "Why I Am a Minister of the Assembly of God."
⁵PDCAG, "Minutes of the Seventh Annual Meeting of the Philippines District Council of the Assemblies of God" (Valenzuela City, Philippines: PGCAG Headquarters Archives, 1949), 3.
⁶Ibid., 4.
⁷PDCAG, "Minutes of the Sixth Annual Convention of the Philippine District Council of the Assemblies of God" (Valenzuela City, Philippines: PGCAG Headquarters Archives, 1948), 3.
⁸Ibid., 4.
⁹Ibid., 3.
¹⁰PDCAG, "Minutes of the Seventh Annual Meeting," 3.
¹¹Rudy C. Esperanza, "Superintendent's Report," *Bulletin*, July 1949, 4.
¹²Rudy C. Esperanza, "District Superintendent's Report," *Bulletin*, March 1951, 7-8.
¹³Rudy C. Esperanza, "Superintendent's Report," *Bulletin*, September 1952, 5.
¹⁴Rudy C. Esperanza, "Superintendent's Report," *Bulletin*, December 1952, 6.
¹⁵Lobarbio stated "eight" districts in the interview. However, the General Secretary's 1965 report lists seven districts. This was reduced to only six districts in the General Secretary's 1967 and 1969 reports. See Rosendo Alcantara, "General Secretary Report" (Valenzuela City, Philippines: PGCAG Headquarters Archives, 1965), 1-2; Rosendo Alcantara, "Report of the General Secretary" (Valenzuela City, Philippines: PGCAG Headquarters Archives, 1967), 1-3; Rosendo Alcantara, "Report of the General Secretary, Eighth General Council Session" (Valenzuela City, Philippines: PGCAG Headquarters Archives, 1969), 1-2. No explanation was given for the reduction in the number of districts. Explanation for the creation and removal of the Central District is given in Johnson, 193-4. To be faithful to the content of the Lobarbio interview, "eight districts" are cited.
¹⁶Lobarbio interview, 16 February 2011, 2.
¹⁷Ibid., 3.
¹⁸Lobarbio pre-video interview, 5.
¹⁹Lobarbio interview, 16 February 2011, 3.
²⁰R. Esperanza, "Why I Am a Minister of the Assembly of God," 2.

[21] Ibid.
[22] R. Esperanza, Diary 1937-1939, 1937 and 1938 entries, *passim*.
[23] Deborah Onggao Lazaro, "My Response to Rosanny Delfin Engcoy's research work as relates to the late Rodrigo C. Esperanza, Sr.," 11 June 2012, email, WA, USA.
[24] Alicia Bautista Tadina, interview by author, 24 March 2011, Pozorrubio, Pangasinan, Philippines, transcript in the hand of author, Rodrigo Esperanza Documentary Project, 1.
[25] R. Esperanza, Diary 1937-1939, May 10, 1939 entry; Bautista interview, 1.
[26] R. Esperanza, Diary 1937-1939, May 1939 entries, *passim*.
[27] R. Esperanza, "Report," March 1951, 6.
[28] Rudy C. Esperanza, "The Church: Its Organizational Structure, Its Relevance to This Hour," *The Pentecostal Voice*, July 1969, 5.
[29] Rudy C. Esperanza, "From the General Superintendent," *Bulletin* January 1954, 3.
[30] Rudy C. Esperanza, "What is Happening in the Philippines," *Bulletin* January 1955, 5.
[31] Lazaro, 11 June 2012, email.
[32] E. Javier interview, 17 February 2011, 6.
[33] Lobarbio pre-video interview, 5.
[34] Rudy C. Esperanza, "District Superintendent's Annual Report," *Bulletin*, April 1951, 10.
[35] Rudy C. Esperanza, "District Superintendent's Annual Report, Seventh Annual Convention," *Bulletin*, April 1949, 14.
[36] R. C. Esperanza, "Superintendent's Report," *Bulletin*, September 1949, 16.
[37] Rudy C. Esperanza, "Ministers Institute," *Bulletin*, October 1951, 16.
[38] Rudy C. Esperanza, "Superintendent's Report," *Bulletin*, May 1952, 8.
[39] R. Esperanza, "What is Happening in the Philippines," 5.
[40] Leonor Esperanza, family newsletter after the death of Rodrigo Esperanza, Rosario, Pozorrubio, Pangasinan, n.d.
[41] Lydia Esperanza Javier and Daniel Esperanza, interview by author, 8 May 2001, Rosario, Pozorrubio, Pangasinan, Philippines, transcript, PGCAG Oral History Collection, Asia Pacific Research Center, Asia Pacific Theological Seminary, Baguio City, Philippines, 10.
[42] Lydia Esperanza Javier, interview by author, 24 March 2011, Pozorrubio, Pangasinan, Philippines, transcript in the hand of author, Rodrigo Esperanza Documentary Project, 7.
[43] E. Javier interview, 17 February 2011, 6.
[44] Ibid.
[45] Ibid.
[46] Darlino Gumallaoi, interview by author, 24 March 2011, Rosario, Pozorrubio, Pangasinan, Philippines, transcript in the hand of author, Rodrigo Esperanza Documentary Project, 1.
[47] E. Javier interview, 17 February 2011, 3. Carmelita A. Gallardo, interview by author, 18 February 2011, Malinta, Valenzuela, Metro Manila, Philippines, transcript in the hand of author, Rodrigo Esperanza Documentary Project, 3.
[48] Irving E. De Mesa, interview by author, 26 July 2012, email, Cavite City, Philippines.
[49] E. Javier interview, 17 February 2011, 7.
[50] Lobarbio pre-video interview, 5.
[51] E. Javier interview, 17 February 2011, 1.
[52] Lazaro, 11 June 2012, email.
[53] Rudy C. Esperanza, "Message," *The Horn 1969*, 5.
[54] The 1964 issue of *The Trumpet*, BBI's school annual, lists Esperanza as Dean and Chairman of the Board of Directors. Harold Kohl was BBI President..
[55] L. Javier interview, 24 March 2011, 6.

184 *Endnotes*

⁵⁶E. Javier interview, 17 February 2011, 1.
⁵⁷De Mesa interview.
⁵⁸Lobarbio pre-video interview, 3.
⁵⁹L. Javier interview, 24 March 2011, 6.
⁶⁰"In Memoriam," *The Trumpet1970*, 5.
⁶¹L. Javier interview, 24 March 2011, 8, 9.
⁶²Lobarbio pre-video interview, 8.
⁶³Petronila Balas, interview by author, 4 March 2011, Baguio City, Philippines, transcript in the hand of author, Rodrigo Esperanza Documentary Project, 3.
⁶⁴Esperanza's 1963 annual report said he accepted the post as BBI President in 1961. He met Lazaro at the Port of Manila in June 1962. The following year, Harold Kohl came to the Philippines and served as BBI President. Subsequently, Esperanza took the post of Academic Dean. Deborah O. Lazaro, email to author, 12 December 2012, WA, USA.
⁶⁵Deborah Lazaro, email to the author, December 12, 2012, WA, USA.
⁶⁶Information in this testimony was taken from Lazaro, 11 June 2012, email.
⁶⁷PDCAG, "Minutes of the First Annual Meeting," 5.
⁶⁸Rebecca Lagmay Alimbuyao, interview by author, 9 March 2011, APTS, Baguio City, Philippines, transcript in the hand of author, Rodrigo Esperanza Documentary Project, 1.
⁶⁹Ibid.

Chapter 7

¹L. Javier and D. Esperanza interview, 4.
²Gumallaoi interview, 3.
³Ibid., 4
⁴Ibid., 5.
⁵Alimbuyao interview, 1-2.
⁶Bautista interview, 3.
⁷Gallardo interview, 4-6.
⁸Ibid., 7.
⁹E. Javier interview, 17 February 2011, 3.
¹⁰Ibid., 7.
¹¹I.e., galvanized steel.
¹²L. Javier interview, 24 March 2011, 4. Speed the Light, a program of the USAG, "is the student-initiated, volunteer, charitable program that provides much-needed equipment to missionaries across the nation and in over 180 countries around the world." "Speed the Light," available at http://stl.ag.org/about/, accessed December 6, 2012.
¹³R. Esperanza, "Report," September 1949, 14.
¹⁴Rudy C. Esperanza, "Superintendent's Report," *Bulletin*, January 1953, 5.
¹⁵E. Javier interview, 17 February 2011, 3. The two Methodist "giants" were Ruben and David Candelaria.
¹⁶E. Javier interview, 17 February 2011, 3.
¹⁷R. Esperanza, Diary 1937-1939.
¹⁸Rudy C. Esperanza, "Report of the General Superintendent to the General Council" (Valenzuela City, Philippines: PGCAG Headquarters Archives, 1963), 1, 2. Esperanza's report has an attached list of the General Superintendent's office furniture and equipments with corresponding prices. Most of the furniture listed is his personal property donated to the office. Also attached is a list of real properties held in the name of PGCAG.
¹⁹Rudy C. Esperanza, "Report of the General Superintendent to the General Council in Session" (Valenzuela City, Philippines: PGCAG Headquarters Archives, 1965), 1.
²⁰E. Javier interview, 17 February 2011, 7.

²¹Lazaro, 11 June 2012, email.
²²PDCAG, "Minutes of the Sixth Annual Convention," 2.
²³R. Esperanza, "Report," May 1952, 3-7.
²⁴R. C. Esperanza, "District Superintendent's Report," *Bulletin*, September 1950, 6.
²⁵Rudy C. Esperanza, "District Superintendent's Report," *Bulletin*, May-June 1951, 5.
²⁶Rudy C. Esperanza, "District Council," *Bulletin*, June 1952, 3-4.
²⁷"Healing and Mass Evangelism," available at http://healingandrevival.com/BioTL Osborn.htm, accessed November 24, 2012.
²⁸Lobarbio interview, 20 January 2006, 14.
²⁹R. Esperanza, "Report of the General Superintendent," 1965, 2.
³⁰R. Esperanza, "Annual Report," April 1949, 8.
³¹Oriel Dumanon, "The Challenge of the Philippines," *Pentecostal Voice*, May 1967, 8.
³² "7th General Council Convention, May 1-5, 1967," *Pentecostal Voice*, May 1967, 13.
³³ Solomon Balimbin, "Editorial Viewpoint: Supporting the Church," *Pentecostal Voice*, May 1967, 4.
³⁴Ibid., 4.
³⁵Rudy C. Esperanza, "Report of the General Superintendent, Eighth General Council Session" (Valenzuela City, Philippines: PGCAG Headquarters Archives, 1969), 2.
³⁶Salvador S. Cayabyab, "The Editorial Voice: Let Us Carry On," *Pentecostal Voice*, December 1969, 2. Esperanza's 1958 diary revealed he was taking insulin shots. Rodrigo Esperanza Diary, January-March 1958, Rodrigo Esperanza Collection, Asia Pacific Research Center, Asia Pacific Theological Seminary, Baguio City, Philippines.
³⁷Lobarbio interview, 16 February 2011, 9-10.
³⁸E. Javier interview, 17 February 2011, 7.
³⁹Lazaro, 11 June 2012, email.
⁴⁰De Mesa interview.
⁴¹Unless otherwise stated, information in this section is from L. Javier interview, 24 March 2011, and L. Javier and D. Esperanza interview, 8 May 2001.
⁴²E. Javier interview, 17 February 2011, 1-2.
⁴³Alimbuyao interview, 1.
⁴⁴Alimbuyao interview, 1, 3.
⁴⁵De Mesa interview.
⁴⁶E. Javier interview, 17 February 2011, 2.
⁴⁷Leonor Esperanza, newsletter.

Chapter 8

¹R. Esperanza, "Report," March 1951, 9.
²Ibid., 9-10.
³R. Esperanza, "The Church," 4; emphasis in original.
⁴Rudy C. Esperanza, "Greetings from the District Superintendent," *Bulletin*, February 1949, 7.
⁵The Pozorrubio church was named "Pentecostal Church" until 1953. Rudy C. Esperanza, "Report of the General Superintendent," *Bulletin*, June 1953, 3.
⁶R. Esperanza, "Greetings," 8.
⁷R. Esperanza, "Annual Report," April 1949, 8.
⁸*Poblacion* - "a center of a municipality in the Philippines that is usually the barrio that gives the municipality its name and is the seat of government," available at http://www.merriam-webster.com/dictionary/poblaci%C3%B3n, accessed November 28, 2012.
⁹R. Esperanza, "Report," July 1949, 3.
¹⁰E. Javier interview, 17 February 2011, 4.

[11] Rudy C. Esperanza, "Superintendent's Report," *Bulletin*, November 1950, 3.
[12] R. Esperanza, "Annual Report," May 1950, 17.
[13] Johnson, 17.
[14] Ibid., 18. The first time the Bible School was referred to as Bethel Bible Institute in the District's official organ was in *Bulletin,* January 1947, 2. However, the resolution giving the District Council Bible school's official name and specifying the members of the school board was presented and approved during the Executive Presbyters and Missionaries Meeting on March 13, 1948. PDCAG, "Minutes of the Sixth Annual Convention," 4
[14] Johnson, 21-35 *passim*.
[15] Tadina interview, 1.
[16] Johnson, 53.
[17] R. Esperanza, "Report," November 1950, 3.
[18] R. Esperanza, "Report," May-June 1951, 6.
[19] R. Esperanza, "Report,"September 1952, 4.
[20] Johnson, 96.
[22] R. Esperanza, "Report," May 1952, 4-5.
[23] Johnson, 99.
[24] R. C. Esperanza, "District Superintendent's Report," *Bulletin,* July 1953, 3.
[25] E. M. and Oneida Brengle, "Immanuel Bible Institute Property Dedicated," *World Challenge,* February 1956, no page.
[26] Scott Shemeth, "Ketcham, Maynard L.," in *NIDPCM*, 821; Maynard L. Ketcham, "Pentecost is on the March in the Far East," *Pentecostal Voice*, October-November 1966, 4. The "additional Bible school" was actually SCBI.
[27] [Rudy C. Esperanza], "The Superintendent Speaks," *Bulletin,* February 1947, 16.
[28] R. Esperanza, "Report," May 1952, 5.
[29] Rudy C. Esperanza, "Superintendent's Report," *Bulletin*, February 1953, 5.
[30] Rudy C. Esperanza, "Let Us March Forward and Advance," *Pentecostal Voice,* June-July 1967, inside back page.
[31] Gumallaoi interview, 3.
[32] Rudy C. Esperanza, "District Superintendent's Report," *Bulletin,* January 1950, 6.
[33] PGCAG, "Philippines General Council of the Assemblies of God, Minutes to the Second General Council Convention" (Valenzuela City, Philippines: PGCAG Headquarters Archives, 1956), 12.
[34] PGCAG, "Philippines General Council, Minutes of the Meeting" (Valenzuela City, Philippines: PGCAG Headquarters Archives, 1963), 2.
[35] Lobarbio interview, 16 February 2011, 3.
[36] Cayabyab, 2.
[37] Rudy C. Esperanza, "Report of the General Superintendent, Seventh General Council in Session" (Valenzuela City, Philippines: PGCAG Headquarters Archives, 1967), 1.
[38] Anacleto Lobarbio, phone interview by author, November 27, 2012. By the time the headquarters was being constructed, Lobarbio was already the Southern Tagalog District Council Presbyter and was privy to the General Presbytery deliberations on the construction plans.
[39] Rudy C. Esperanza, "Ways and Means: Gospel Literature," *Pentecostal Voice,* October 1965, 9.
[40] Robert Malone, "The Assemblies of God and Its Program of Literature: Production and Distribution," *Pentecostal Voice,* October 1965, 7.
[41] See "Background and Birth of the PGCAG," p. 40.
[42] R. Esperanza, "Report," November 1950, 4-5.
[43] David Daniels III, "African-American Pentecostalism in the 20th Century," in *The Century of the Holy Spirit: 100 Years of Pentecostal and Charismatic Renewal, 1901-2001*, ed. Vinson Synan (Nashville, TN: Thomas Nelson, 2001), 274.

⁴⁴Robert Owens, "The Azusa Street Revival: The Pentecostal Movement Begins in America," in Synan, *The Century of the Holy Spirit*, 62.

⁴⁵"The Editor Testifies," *Bulletin*, January 1947, 1.

⁴⁶PGCAG, "Second General Council Convention," 14. The Literature Department (Committee) was formed during the same Convention.

⁴⁷Narciso Dionson, text messages, 18 December 2012, Aklan, Philippines. Dionson was the last editor of the *Pentecostal Voice*. He was editor for two years, then publication of the magazine was stopped.

⁴⁸Sanneh, 90.

⁴⁹R. C. Esperanza, "The District Council: God is Doing a New Thing in the Philippines," *Bulletin*, October 1950, 4.

⁵⁰Ibid., 4-5.

⁵¹See "Background and Birth of the PGCAG," p. 43.

⁵²R. Esperanza, "Annual Report," April 1951, 9-10.

⁵³Johnson, 73.

⁵⁴R. Esperanza, "Ways and Means," 9.

⁵⁵Ibid.

⁵⁶Rudy C. Esperanza, "District Council," *Bulletin*, July 1952, 5.

⁵⁷R. Esperanza, "Report," May 1952, 5-6.

⁵⁸R. Esperanza, "Ways and Means," 9.

⁵⁹Ibid.

⁶⁰R. Esperanza, "Report," May 1952, 6.

⁶¹R. Esperanza, "Ways and Means," 9; Johnson, 149.

⁶²Malone, 7.

⁶³Maynard Ketcham, "Pentecostal Revivals Continue to Girdle Around the World," *Pentecostal Voice*, May 1967, 18.

⁶⁴PDCAG, "Philippines District Council of the Assemblies of God, Minutes of the Ninth Annual Convention" (Valenzuela City, Philippines: PGCAG Headquarters Archives, 1951), 4.

⁶⁵Calvin R. Zeissler, "Profiles in Literature: Let Us Support Our Literature Program," *Pentecostal Voice*, May 1967, 10; emphasis in original.

⁶⁶R. Esperanza, "Eighth General Council Session," 2; emphasis in original.

⁶⁷PGCAG, "Business Session, Minutes of the Philippines General Council Convention" (Valenzuela City, Philippines: PGCAG Headquarters Archives, 1959), 11; typographical and grammatical errors in the original.

⁶⁸Johnson, 153.

⁶⁹Among its various ministries, ICI "publish[es] literatures for Christian growth." "ICI Ministries Philippines," available at http://www.iciphilippines.org/site/ici.php?section=history, accessed December 6, 2012. APMM "is the regional media ministry for the Assemblies of God World Missions." "Asia Pacific Media Ministries," available at http://www.agwmphilippines.org/ministry.php?name=Asia_Pacific_Media_Ministries, accessed December 6, 2012.

⁷⁰R. Esperanza, "The Church," 5.

⁷¹R. Esperanza, "Report," September 1949, 13.

⁷²Johnson, 60, 157.

⁷³PGCAG, "Minutes to the Sixth General Council Convention of the Philippines General Council of the Assemblies of God" (Valenzuela City, Philippines: PGCAG Headquarters Archives, 1965), 5.

⁷⁴R. Esperanza, "Let Us March Forward and Advance," inside back page. The CA was the first national youth organization of the USAG started in 1926; "Assemblies of God News," available at http://rss.ag.org/articles/detail.cfm?RSS_RSSContentID=24138&RSS_OriginatingChannelID=1184&RSS_OriginatingRSSFeedID=3359&RSS_Source=rssFile_3359, accessed December 16, 2012.

⁷⁵Lobarbio interview, 20 January 2006, 5.

[76] Ibid. The year 2004 was texted by Anacleto Lobarbio to the author, December 6, 2012.
[77] Rudy C. Esperanza, "Superintendent's Report," *Bulletin*, November-December 1949, 10.
[78] Rudy C. Esperanza, "District Superintendent's Report," *Bulletin*, June-July 1951, 7.
[79] "News Reports," *Bulletin*, October 1952, 6.
[80] "News Reports," *Bulletin*, June 1950, 6.
[81] Aurelio Gonzales, "A New Assembly was Born Thru the Ministry of Radio," *Pentecostal Voice*, July 1966, 17.
[82] R. Esperanza, "Let Us March Forward and Advance," inside back page.
[83] R. Esperanza, "Report," September 1950, 5.
[84] R. Esperanza, "Report of the General Superintendent," 1965, 3; emphasis in the original.
[85] PGCAG, "Sixth General Council Convention," 13.
[86] "BBI Spearheads Foreign Missions Drive," *Pentecostal Voice*, October 1965, 12.
[87] "Southern Luzon District Holds First Mission Rally," *Pentecostal Voice*, October-November 1966, 6.
[88] [Solomon Balimbin], "Editorial Comment: A Challenge to Act Now!" *Pentecostal Voice*, August 1966, 11.
[89] "Every Christian a Missionary," *Pentecostal Voice*, May 1967, 9.
[90] Eliseo M. Sadorra, "Asian Missionary Fact-Finding Report," *Pentecostal Voice*, June 1969, 10-11, 13.
[91] "8th General Council Convention of the Assemblies of God," program brochure (Valenzuela City, Philippines: PGCAG Headquarters Archives, 1969), back page.
[92] "General Council Boosts Missions," *Pentecostal Voice*, June 1969, 8-9.
[93] R. Esperanza, "Eighth General Council Session" 2-3.
[94] Cayabyab, 2.
[95] Lazaro, 11 June 2012, email.
[96] Ma, 202.
[97] "World Missions Department, Philippines General Council of the Assemblies of God," available at http://pgcagwmd.wordpress.com/, accessed December 7, 2012.

Chapter 9

[1] E. Javier interview, 17 February 2011, 6, 7.
[2] R. Esperanza, "Report," May 1952, 7.
[3] R. Esperanza, "Report of the General Superintendent," 1963, 1.
[4] R. Esperanza, "Report of the General Superintendent," 1965, 1.
[5] R. Esperanza, "Let Us March Forward and Advance," inside front cover.
[6] R. Esperanza, "Eighth General Council Session," 1-4.
[7] R. Esperanza, "Report of the General Superintendent," 1965, 3.
[8] "Constitution and By-Laws of the General Council of the Assemblies of God Including Essential Resolutions Revised and Adopted, September 16-22, 1927," 3-4, Flower Pentecostal Heritage Center CD Collection, Asia Pacific Research Center, Asia Pacific Theological Seminary, Baguio City, Philippines.
[9] R. Esperanza, "Annual Report," May 1950, 15.
[10] R. Esperanza, "Report," May 1952, 4.
[11] See "Background and Birth of the PGCAG," p. 48.
[12] [Rudy C. Esperanza], Report of the General Superintendent, General Council Session Minutes (Valenzuela City, Philippines: PGCAG Headquarters Archives, 1956), 1.
[13] Gallardo interview, 8.
[14] Dumanon, 8.

[15] PGCAG, "Seventh General Convention, Philippines General Council of the Assemblies of God Minutes" (Valenzuela City, Philippines: PGCAG Headquarters Archives, 1967), 2.
[16] Johnson, 125.
[17] R. Esperanza, "Eighth General Council Session," 3.
[18] Unless otherwise stated, information on this conflict is from Johnson, Chapter 14, "Schism, Split and Healing." For a more detailed treatment of this topic, see source.
[19] E. Javier interview, 17 February 2011, 2.
[20] PAG records in the APRC archives give the name as "Philippine Assemblies of God."
[21] E. Javier interview, 17 February 2011, 2-3.
[22] For more information on these events from 1969 to 1979, see Johnson, chapter 14.
[23] Johnson, 125.
[24] Agoncillo, 330.
[26] E. Javier, "The Pentecostal Legacy," 73.
[27] Later called Assemblies of God World Missions or AGWM.
[28] PGCAG, "Proposed Amendments and Additions to the Constitution" (Valenzuela City, Philippines: PGCAG Headquarters Archives, 1959), 1; italics mine.
[29] PGCAG, "Business Session," 13. In May 1961, the PGCAG General Presbytery decided that missionaries were no longer needed to serve as district or general superintendent. "Minutes of the General Presbyters' Meeting, May 1, 1961;" quoted in Johnson, 119.
[30] PGCAG, "Business Session," 14.
[31] Johnson, 119.
[32] Ibid., 121-2.
[33] Rudy C. Esperanza, "Leadership and Coordination Conferences," *Pentecostal Voice*, February-March 1968, 4.
[34] Derrick Hillary, "Thinking Out Loud," letter to the missionaries of the AGMF, March 1968; quoted in Johnson, 124.
[35] E. Javier interview, 17 February 2011, 2.
[36] Johnson, 127.
[37] Gallardo interview, 3.
[38] PGCAG, "Philippines General Council Minutes," 1963, 2.
[39] Gallardo interview, 3-4.
[40] PGCAG, "Philippines General Council Minutes," 1963, 4.
[41] Gallardo interview, 9.
[42] R. Esperanza, "Annual Report," May 1950, 15.
[42] Gallardo interview, 6.
[43] Ibid., 13.

Chapter 10

[1] Esperanza did not mention the year, but the crusade was most probably held March 10 to 17, 1963, based on Ernesto Montalbo Cruz's book, *An Evaluation of Decisions Made at the All-Philippines Billy Graham Crusade Held March 10 to 17, 1963 in Manila, Philippines*; available at http://books.google.com.ph/books/about/An_Evaluation_of_Decisions_Made_at_the_A.html?id=RmHLNwAACAAJ&redir_esc=y, accessed January 11, 2013.
[2] CHED, the Commission on Higher Education, "is responsible in the formulation and implementation of policies, plans and programs for the development and efficient operation of the higher education system in the [Philippines]," available at http://www.ched.gov.ph/chedwww/index.php/eng/Information, accessed January 4, 2013.

³Dr. John Carter was APTS President when I studied there from 1996 to 1998. He was still President when I returned to the seminary in June 2000.

⁴"Why Study Church History?" available at http://www.christianitytoday.com/ch/1990/issue25/2541.html, accessed January 11, 2013.

BIBLIOGRAPHY

Achutegui, Pedro S. de, and Miguel A. Bernad. *Religious Revolution in the Philippines: The Life and Church of Gregorio Aglipay.* Manila: Ateneo de Manila, 1966.
Agoncillo, Teodoro A. *History of the Filipino People*, 8th ed. Quezon City, Philippines: Garotech Publishing, 1999.
Alcantara, Rosendo. "General Secretary Report." Valenzuela City, Philippines: PGCAG Headquarters Archives, 1965.
_____. "Report of the General Secretary." Valenzuela City, Philippines: PGCAG Headquarters Archives, 1967.
_____. "Report of the General Secretary, Eighth General Council Session." Valenzuela City, Philippines: PGCAG Headquarters Archives, 1969.
Alcantara, Rosendo and Presentacion. First Interview. Interview by author, 4 July 2001, Bakersfield, CA. Transcript. PGCAG Oral History Collection, Asia Pacific Research Center, Asia Pacific Theological Seminary, Baguio City, Philippines.
_____. 2nd Interview. Interview by author, 7 July 2001, Bakersfield, CA. Transcript. PGCAG Oral History Collection, Asia Pacific Research Center, Asia Pacific Theological Seminary, Baguio City, Philippines.
Alimbuyao, Rebecca Lagmay. Interview by author, 9 March 2011, Asia Pacific Theological Seminary, Baguio City, Philippines. Transcript in the hand of author. Rodrigo Esperanza Documentary Project.
Anderson, Allan. *An Introduction to Pentecostalism.* Cambridge: Cambridge University Press, 2004.
Anderson, Gerald H. "Providence and Politics behind Protestant Missionary Beginnings in the Philippines." In *Studies in Philippine Church History*, ed. Gerald H. Anderson, 279-300. London: Cornell University Press, 1969.
Anderson, Robert Mapes. *Vision of the Disinherited: The Making of American Pentecostalism.* Oxford: Oxford University Press, 1979.
Apilado, Mariano C. "The United Church of Christ in the Philippines: Historical Location, Theological Roots, and Spiritual Commitment." In *Chapters in Philippine Church History*, ed. Anne C. Kwantes, 335-58. Manila, Philippines: OMF Literature, 2001.
_____. *Revolutionary Spirituality: A Study of the Protestant Role in the American Colonial Rule of the Philippines, 1898-1928.* Quezon City, Philippines: New Day, 1999.
Aragon, Averell U. "The Philippine Council of Evangelical Churches." In *Chapters in Philippine Church History*, ed. Anne C. Kwantes, 369-389. Manila, Philippines: OMF Literature, 2001.
Aragona, Angela Salazar. Interview by author, 14 April 2002, Iloilo City, Philippines. Transcript. Oral History Collection, Asia Pacific Research Center, Asia Pacific Theological Seminary, Baguio City, Philippines.
Arangote, Marcelo. Interview by author, 23 April 2003, Bethel Bible College Campus, Malinta, Valenzuela, MM, Philippines. Transcript. Oral History Collection, Asia Pacific Research Center, Asia Pacific Theological Seminary, Baguio City, Philippines.
"Asia Pacific Media Ministries." Available at http://www.agwmphilippines.org/ministry.php?name=Asia_Pacific_Media_Ministries, accessed December 6, 2012.
"Assemblies of God Beginnings." *Focus-Philippines.* USAG Missionary Pioneers. Dave Johnson Archives, Asia Pacific Research Center, Asia Pacific Theological Seminary, Baguio City, Philippines.

"Assemblies of God News." Available at
http://rss.ag.org/articles/detail.cfm?RSS_RSSContentID=24138&RSS_OriginatingCh
annelID=1184&RSS_OriginatingRSSFeedID=3359&RSS_Source=rssFile_3359,
accessed December 16, 2012.
Balas, Petronila. Interview by author, 4 March 2011, Baguio City, Philippines. Transcript
in the hand of author. Rodrigo Esperanza Documentary Project.
[Balimbin, Solomon.] "Editorial Comment: A Challenge to Act Now!" *Pentecostal Voice*, August 1966, 11.
_____. "Editorial Viewpoint: Supporting the Church." *Pentecostal Voice*, May 1967, 4.
Barrett, David B., ed. *World Christian Encyclopedia: A Comparative Survey of Churches and Religions in the Modern World, A.D. 1900-2000*. Oxford: Oxford University Press, 1982.
Bartleman, Frank. *Azusa Street: The Roots of Modern-Day Pentecost*. With an introduction by Vinson Synan. South Plainfield, NJ: Bridge Publishing, 1980.
Bautista, Jesse. Interview by author, 24 March 2011, Pozorrubio, Pangasinan, Philippines. Handwritten notes in the hand of author, Rodrigo Esperanza Documentary Project.
_____. Interview by author, 24 March 2011, Pozorrubio, Pangasinan, Philippines. Transcript in the hand of author, Rodrigo Esperanza Documentary Project.
"*Bayanihan.*" Available at http://groups.csail.mit.edu/cag/bayanihan/bayanword.html, accessed December 15, 2012.
"BBI Spearheads Foreign Missions Drive." *Pentecostal Voice*, October 1965, 12, 27.
Bell, E. N., ed. "General Convention of Pentecostal Saints and Churches of God in Christ." *Word and Witness,* 20 December 1913, 1. Flower Pentecostal Heritage Center CD Collection, Asia Pacific Research Center, Asia Pacific Theological Seminary, Baguio City, Philippines.
_____, ed. "Hot Springs Assembly; God's Glory Present." *Word and Witness,* 20 April 1914, 1. Flower Pentecostal Heritage Center CD Collection, Asia Pacific Research Center, Asia Pacific Theological Seminary, Baguio City, Philippines.
Biehl, Bobb. *Mentoring: Confidence in Finding a Mentor and Becoming One*. Nashville, TN: Broadman & Holman, 1996.
Blumhofer, Edith L. *The Assemblies of God: A Chapter in the Story of American Pentecostalism*. 2 vols. Springfield, MO: Gospel Publishing House, 1989.
_____. *Pentecost in My Soul: Explorations in the Meaning of Pentecostal Experience in the Early Assemblies of God.* Springfield, MO: Gospel Publishing House, 1989.
_____. *Restoring the Faith: The Assemblies of God, Pentecostalism, and American Culture*. Chicago: University of Illinois Press, 1993.
Boyd, Gregory A. *Oneness Pentecostals and the Trinity*. Grand Rapids, MI: Baker, 1992.
Brengle, E. M., and Oneida Brengle. "Immanuel Bible Institute Property Dedicated." *World Challenge*, February 1956, no page.
"Brief Historical Perspective of the Philippine General Council of the Assemblies of God." *Intercom*, June 1994.
Brumback, Carl. *Suddenly...from Heaven: A History of the Assemblies of God*. Springfield, MO: Gospel Publishing House, 1961.
Bulatao, Jaime. "The 'Hiya' System in Filipino Culture." In *Filipino Cultural Heritage*, ed. F. Landa Jocano. Filipino Social Structure and Value Orientation, no. 2, 27-41. Manila, Philippines: Philippine Women's University, 1966.
Bunda, Nestor Distor. *A Mission History of the Philippine Baptist Churches 1898-1998 from a Philippine Perspective*. Aachen, Germany: Verlag an der Lottbek im Besitz des Verlags Mainz, 1999.
Burgess, Stanley, ed. *The New International Dictionary of Pentecostal and Charismatic Movements*, rev. and exp. ed. Grand Rapids, MI: Zondervan, 2002.

Cagas, Roque Sr., and Estrella Cagas. Interview by author, 11 April 2002, Talisay, Cebu, Philippines. Transcript. PGCAG Oral History Collection, Asia Pacific Research Center, Asia Pacific Theological Seminary, Baguio City, Philippines.

Carlson, G. Raymond, D. V. Hurst, and Cyril E. Homer. *The Assemblies of God in Mission.* Springfield, MO: Gospel Publishing House, 1970.

Caudle, Benjamin H. "Application for Appointment as Missionary by the Foreign Missions Department, General Council of the Assemblies of God, April 28, 1924." USAG Missionary Pioneers. Dave Johnson Archives, Asia Pacific Research Center, Asia Pacific Theological Seminary, Baguio City, Philippines.

_____. "Opportunities in Manila, 8.27.27," and "Manila, Philippine Islands, 3.10.28," USAG Missionary Pioneers. Dave Johnson Archives, Asia Pacific Research Center, Asia Pacific Theological Seminary, Baguio City.

Cayabyab, Salvador S. "The Editorial Voice: Let Us Carry On." *Pentecostal Voice*, December 1969, 2.

Cerillo, Augustus Jr., and Grant Wacker. "Bibliography and Historiography of Pentecostalism in the United States." In *The New International Dictionary of Pentecostal and Charismatic Movements*, rev. and exp. ed., ed. Stanley Burgess, 382-405. Grand Rapids, MI: Zondervan, 2002.

Clymer, Kenton J. "Protestant Missionaries and American Colonialism in the Philippines, 1899-1916: Attitudes, Perceptions, Involvement." In *Reappraising an Empire: New Perspectives on Philippine American History*, ed. Peter W. Stanley, 143-70. Cambridge, MA: Harvard University Press, 1984.

_____. *Protestant Missionaries in the Philippines, 1898-1916: An Inquiry into the American Colonial Mentality.* Chicago: University of Illinois Press, 1986.

Colcolen, Narciso. Interview by author, 15 April 2003, Bussot, Gregorio del Pilar, Ilocos Sur, Philippines. Transcript. Oral History Collection, Asia Pacific Research Center, Asia Pacific Theological Seminary, Baguio City, Philippines.

Collins, Gary R. *Christian Coaching: Helping Others Turn Potential into Reality.* Colorado Springs, CO: NavPress, 2001.

Conn, Charles W. *Like a Mighty Army: Moves the Church of God 1886-1955.* Cleveland, TN: Church of God Publishing House, 1955.

_____. *Where the Saints Have Trod: A History of Church of God Missions.* Cleveland, TN: Pathway Press, 1959.

Constantino, Renato. *The Philippines: A Past Revisited.* Quezon City, Philippines: Renato Constantino, 1975.

Constitution and By-Laws of the General Council of the Assemblies of God Including Essential Resolutions Revised and Adopted, September 16-22, 1927. Flower Pentecostal Heritage Center CD Collection, Asia Pacific Research Center, Asia Pacific Theological Seminary, Baguio City, Philippines.

Cox, Harvey. *Fire from Heaven: The Rise of Pentecostal Spirituality and the Reshaping of Religion in the Twenty-first Century.* Reading, MA: Addison-Wesley, 1995.

Cunningham, Floyd T. *Examining Our Christian Heritage 2, Faculty Guide.* Kansas City, MO: Church of the Nazarene Clergy Development, 2004.

Cruz, Ernesto Montalbo. *An Evaluation of Decisions Made at the All-Philippines Billy Graham Crusade Held March 10 to 17, 1963 in Manila, Philippines.* Available at http://books.google.com.ph/books/about/An_Evaluation_of_Decisions_Made_at_th e_A.html?id=RmHLNwAACAAJ&redir_esc=y, accessed January 11, 2013.

Daniels, David, III. "African-American Pentecostalism in the 20th Century." In *The Century of the Holy Spirit: 100 Years of Pentecostal and Charismatic Renewal, 1901-2001*, ed. Vinson Synan. Nashville, TN: Thomas Nelson, 2001.

Dayton, Donald W. *Theological Roots of Pentecostalism.* Grand Rapids, MI: Zondervan, 1987. Reprint, Peabody, MA: Hendrickson, 1994.

De Mesa, Irving E. Interview by author, 26 July 2012. Email, Cavite City, Philippines.

Delmendo, Sharon. *The Star-Entangled Banner*. Quezon City, Philippines: University of the Philippines Press, 2005.
Denton, James. Interview by author, 11 August 2001, Transcript. APRC Oral History Collection, Asia Pacific Research Center, Asia Pacific Theological Seminary, Baguio City, Philippines.
Diel, Domingo J. Jr. "Perspective on Baptist Church History." In *Chapters in Philippine Church History,* ed. Anne C. Kwantes, 225-37. Manila, Philippines: OMF Literature, 2001.
Dieter, Melvin Easterly. *The Holiness Revival of the Nineteenth Century*. Metuchen, NJ: Scarecrow Press, 1980.
Dionson, Narciso. Text messages, 18 December 2012, Aklan, Philippines.
Dumanon, Oriel. "The Challenge of the Philippines." *Pentecostal Voice*, May 1967, 8, 12.
"The Editor Testifies," *Bulletin*, January 1947, 1.
"8th General Council Convention of the Assemblies of God." Program brochure. Valenzuela City, Philippines: PGCAG Headquarters Archives, 1969.
Esperanza, Daniel. Handwritten list of positions held by R. C. Esperanza, n.d.
Esperanza, Dionisio. "R. C. Esperanza: Early life events as told by his father." N.d.
Esperanza, Leonor. Family newsletter after the death of Rodrigo Esperanza, Rosario, Pozorrubio, Pangasinan, nd.
Esperanza, R. C. "The District Council: God is Doing a New Thing in the Philippines." *Bulletin,* October 1950, 3-6.
_____. "District Superintendent's Report." *Bulletin*, June 1950, 2-5.
_____. "District Superintendent's Report." *Bulletin*, September 1950, 5-6.
_____. "Superintendent's Report." *Bulletin*, September 1949, 14-16.
_____. "Why I Am a Minister of the Assembly of God." Rodolfo Esperanza Collection, Asia Pacific Research Center, Asia Pacific Theological Seminary, Baguio City, Philippines.
[Esperanza Rodrigo C.] Affidavit, 14 August 1946. Valenzuela City, Philippines: PGCAG Headquarters Archives, 1967.
_____. Diary 1937-1939. Rodrigo Esperanza Collection, Asia Pacific Research Center Archives, Asia Pacific Theological Seminary, Baguio City, Philippines.
_____. Ledgers, 1941-1952. Rodrigo Esperanza Collection, Asia Pacific Research Center, Asia Pacific Theological Seminary, Baguio City, Philippines.
_____. "Report of the General Superintendent." *Bulletin,* June 1953, 3.
Esperanza, Rudy C. The Church: Its Organizational Structure, Its Relevance to This Hour," *Pentecostal Voice*, July 1969, 4-5.
_____. Diary, January-March 1958. Rodrigo Esperanza Collection, Asia Pacific Research Center Archives, Asia Pacific Theological Seminary, Baguio City, Philippines.
_____. "District Council." *Bulletin*, July 1952, 4-5.
_____. "District Council." *Bulletin*, June 1952, 3-4.
_____. "District Superintendent's Annual Report, Seventh Annual Convention April 12-15, 1949." *Bulletin*, April 1949, 7,8,14,15.
_____. "District Superintendent's Annual Report." *Bulletin*, April 1951, 9-14.
_____. "District Superintendent's Annual Report." *Bulletin*, May 1950, 15-18.
_____. "District Superintendent's Report." *Bulletin*, March 1951, 6-10.
_____. "District Superintendent's Report." *Bulletin*, May-June 1951, 5-6.
_____. "District Superintendent's Report." *Bulletin*, June-July 1951, 5-7.
_____. "District Superintendent's Report." *Bulletin*, January 1950, 6-7.
_____. "District Superintendent's Report." *Bulletin*, February 1950, 7-9.
_____. "From the General Superintendent." *Bulletin* January 1954, 3.
_____. "General Superintendent's Report." *Bulletin*, July 1953, 3-4.
_____. "Greetings from the District Superintendent." *Bulletin*, February 1949, 6-8.

_____. "Leadership and Coordination Conferences." *Pentecostal Voice*, February-March 1968, 3-4.
_____. "Let Us March Forward and Advance." *Pentecostal Voice*, June-July 1967, inside front cover and inside back page.
_____. "Message." *The Horn*, 1969.
_____. "Ministers Institute." *Bulletin*, October 1951, 13, 16.
_____. "The Need in the Philippine Islands." *Missionary Challenge*, July 1948, 15.
[_____.] "Report of the General Superintendent, General Council Session Minutes." Valenzuela City, Philippines: PGCAG Headquarters Archives, 1956.
_____. "Report of the General Superintendent to the General Council." Valenzuela City, Philippines: PGCAG Headquarters Archives, 1963.
_____. "Report of the General Superintendent to the General Council in Session." Valenzuela City, Philippines: PGCAG Headquarters Archives, 1965.
_____. "Report of the General Superintendent, Eighth General Council Session." Valenzuela City, Philippines: PGCAG Headquarters Archives, 1969.
_____. "Report of the General Superintendent, Seventh General Council in Session." Valenzuela City, Philippines: PGCAG Headquarters Archives, 1967.
_____. "Superintendent's Report." *Bulletin*, December 1952, 6-8, 11.
_____. "Superintendent's Report." *Bulletin*, February 1953, 5-7.
_____. "Superintendent's Report." *Bulletin*, January 1953, 4-5.
_____. "Superintendent's Report." *Bulletin*, July 1949, 3-4.
_____. "Superintendent's Report." *Bulletin*, May 1952, 3-7.
_____. "Superintendent's Report." *Bulletin*, November 1950, 3-6.
_____. "Superintendent's Report." *Bulletin*, November-December 1949, 10, 15.
_____. "Superintendent's Report." *Bulletin*, September 1952, 4-5.
[_____.] "The Superintendent Speaks." *Bulletin*, February 1947, 16-18.
_____. "Ways and Means: Gospel Literature." *Pentecostal Voice*, October 1965, 9.
_____. "Welcome-Bethel to the Philippines." *Bulletin*, August 1951, 10.
_____. "What is Happening in the Philippines." *Bulletin*, January 1955, 4-5.
Esperanza, Trinidad C. "The Assemblies of God in the Philippines." MRE thesis, Fuller Theological Seminary, 1965.
"Every Christian a Missionary." *Pentecostal Voice*, May 1967, 9.
"The Founder and Church History: 'The Church of God in Christ.'" Available at www.cogic.org/our-foundation/the-founder-church-history/, accessed February 7, 2013.
Foursquare History and Distinctives. Manila, Philippines: Church of the Foursquare Gospel in the Philippines Department of Advanced Christian Education, 1998.
Gallardo, Carmelita A. Interview by author, 18 February 2011, Southern Tagalog District Council Office, Bethel Bible College Campus, Malinta, Valenzuela, MM, Philippines. Transcript in the hand of author. Rodrigo Esperanza Documentary Project.
Garsulao, Mamerto, to Rosanny D. Engcoy, 12 December 2002. Philippines Filipino Assemblies of God Pioneers. Asia Pacific Research Center, Asia Pacific Theological Seminary, Baguio City, Philippines.
Garsulao, Mamerto. Interview by author, 18 April 2002, Iloilo City, Philippines. Transcript. PGCAG Oral History Collection, Asia Pacific Research Center, Asia Pacific Theological Seminary, Baguio City, Philippines.
Gee, Donald. *The Pentecostal Movement*, enl. ed. London: Elim, 1949.
"General Council Boosts Missions." *Pentecostal Voice*, June 1969, 8-9.
Glad Tidings Articles, News clippings. Department of Foreign Missions Archives, USAG Headquarters, Springfield, MO:
"Another Graduate Left for the Foreign Field." February 1928, 9.
"Antique, P.I." March 1934, 12.
"In the Service of the King." June 1933, 8.

"In the Service of the King: Sibalem [sic], Antique, P.I." May 1928, 8.
"Promoted to Glory," March 1935, 2-1.
"Sebalom[sic], Antique, P. I." November 1930, 10.
Goff, James R. Jr. "Parham, Charles Fox." In *The New International Dictionary of Pentecostal and Charismatic Movements*, rev. and exp. ed., ed. Stanley Burgess, 955-7. Grand Rapids, MI: Zondervan, 2002.
_____. "Sanctification Scuffles." *Christian History*, no. 58, 18-19.
Gonzales, Aurelio. "A New Assembly was Born Thru the Ministry of Radio." *Pentecostal Voice*, July 1966, 17.
Gonzales, Mariano. Interview by author, 8 May 2003, San Nicolas, Ilocos Norte, Philippines. Transcript. PGCAG Oral History Collection, Asia Pacific Research Center, Asia Pacific Theological Seminary, Baguio City, Philippines.
Gonzalez, Justo L. *The Story of Christianity.* Vol. 2, *The Reformation to the Present Day.* New York: Harper and Row, 1985.
Gowing, Peter G. *Islands Under the Cross: The Story of the Church in the Philippines.* Manila, Philippines: National Council of Churches in the Philippines, 1967.
Gumallaoi, Darlino. Interview by author, 24 March 2011, Rosario, Pozorrubio, Pangasinan, Philippines. Transcript in the hand of author. Rodrigo Esperanza Documentary Project.
"Healing and Mass Evangelism." Available at http://healingandrevival.com/BioTLOsborn.htm, accessed November 24, 2012.
Hollenweger, Walter J. *Pentecostalism: Origins and Developments Worldwide.* Peabody, MA: Hendrickson, 1997.
_____. *The Pentecostals.* Translated by R. A. Wilson. London: SCM, 1972.
Hwa Yung. "Pentecostalism and the Asian Church." In *Asian and Pentecostal: The Charismatic Face of Christianity in Asia*, eds. Allan Anderson and Edmond Tang. Regnum Studies in Mission/Asian Journal of Pentecostal Studies Series 3, 37-57. Baguio City, Philippines: APTS Press, 2005.
"ICI Ministries Philippines." Available at http://www.iciphilippines.org/site/ici.php?section=history, accessed December 6, 2012.
"In Memoriam." *The Trumpet 1970.* Bethel Bible College school annual.
"The International Assemblies of the First Born." Available at http://www.iafb.us/history.html, accessed December 4, 2012.
Jacobsen, Douglas. *Thinking in the Spirit: Theologies of the Early Pentecostal Movement.* Indianapolis, IN: Indiana University Press, 2003.
Javier, Eleazer E. "A Brief History of the Messiah Community Church (Formerly the Taytay Methodist Community Church)." January 2007.
_____. Conversation with author, 10 March 2005, Taytay, Rizal, Philippines. Transcript. PGCAG Oral History Collection, Asia Pacific Research Center, Asia Pacific Theological Seminary, Baguio City, Philippines.
_____. First Interview. Interview by author, 15 September 2001, ICS, Mandaluyong City, MM, Philippines. Transcript. Oral History Collection, Asia Pacific Research Center, Asia Pacific Theological Seminary, Baguio City, Philippines.
_____. Interview by author, 17 February 2011, Taytay, Rizal, Philippines. Transcript in hand of author. Rodrigo Esperanza Documentary Project.
_____. "Our Pentecostal Legacy." Lecture, 15 September 2001, ICS, Mandaluyong City, MM, Philippines. Oral History Collection, Asia Pacific Research Center, Asia Pacific Theological Seminary, Baguio City, Philippines.
_____. "The Pentecostal Legacy." In *Supplement to Chapters in Philippine Church History*, ed. Anne C. Kwantes, 57-82. Manila, Philippines: OMF Literature, 2002.
Javier, Esther Candelaria. Interview by author, 10 March 2005, Taytay, Rizal, Philippines. Transcript. PGCAG Oral History Collection, Asia Pacific Research Center, Asia Pacific Theological Seminary, Baguio City, Philippines.

Javier, Lydia Esperanza, and Daniel Esperanza. Interview by author, 8 May 2001, Rosario, Pozzorubio, Pangasinan, Philippines. Transcript. PGCAG Oral History Collection, Asia Pacific Research Center, Asia Pacific Theological Seminary, Baguio City, Philippines.
Javier, Lydia Esperanza. Interview by author, 24 March 2011, Pozorrubio, Pangasinan, Philippines. Transcript in the hand of author. Rodrigo Esperanza Documentary Project.
Joaquin, Nick. *Culture and History*. Mandaluyong City, Philippines: Anvil Publishing, 2004.
Jocano, F. Landa. "Filipino Social Structure and Value System." In *Filipino Cultural Heritage*, ed. F. Landa Jocano. Filipino Social Structure and Value Orientation, no. 2, 1-26. Manila, Philippines: Philippine Women's University, 1966.
Johnson, Dave. *Led by the Spirit: The History of the American Assemblies of God Missionaries in the Philippines*. Pasig City, Philippines: ICI Ministries, 2009.
Kay, William K. *Pentecostalism*. London: SCM Press, 2009.
Kendrick, Klaude. *The Promise Fulfilled: A History of the Modern Pentecostal Movement*. Springfield, MO: Gospel Publishing House, 1961.
Kennedy, John W. "The Philippines: Embracing the Challenge." *Pentecostal Evangel*, 4 June 2000, 5.
Ketcham, Maynard L. "Pentecost is on the March in the Far East." *Pentecostal Voice*, October-November 1966, 4-5.
_____. "Pentecostal Revivals Continue to Girdle Around the World." *Pentecostal Voice*, May 1967, 17-18, 20.
Kipling, Rudyard. Available at "The White Man's Burden." http://www.online-literature.com/keats/922/, accessed February 11, 2012.
Kwantes, Anne C. "Presbyterian Missionaries in the Philippines: A Historical Analysis of their Contributions to Social Change (1899-1910)." Ph.D. diss., University of the Philippines, 1988.
Lanphear, L. E. "Philippines Radio Outreach." *Pentecostal Voice*, April 1966, 16-17.
"Largest Denominations: Philippines." *DAWN Philippines: A Report on the State of the Evangelical Churches in the Philippines 2000*. With a foreword by Bishop Efraim M. Tendero. N.p. and n.d., 40.
Laubach, Frank Charles. *The People of the Philippines: Their Religious Progress and Preparation for Spiritual Leadership in the Far East*. New York: George H. Duran, 1925.
Lazaro, Deborah Onggao. Email to author, 12 December 2012, WA, USA.
_____. "My Response to Rosanny Delfin Engcoy's research work as relates to the late Rodrigo C. Esperanza, Sr." 11 June 2012. Email. WA, USA.
Lim, Pedro. Interview by author, 20 December 2005. Transcript. APRC Oral History Collection, Asia Pacific Research Center, Asia Pacific Theological Seminary, Baguio City, Philippines.
"Link Interview: Pentecostalism's Global Language: An Interview with Walter J. Hollenweger." *Christian History* 17, no. 58 (1998): 42.
Lobarbio, Anacleto. Interview by author, 16 February 2011, Pasig City, MM, Philippines. Transcript in the hand of author, Rodrigo Esperanza Documentary Project.
_____. Interview by author, 20 January 2006, Pasig City, MM, Philippines. Transcript. PGCAG Oral History Collection, Asia Pacific Research Center, Asia Pacific Theological Seminary, Baguio City, Philippines.
_____. Phone interview by author, November 27, 2012.
_____. Pre-Video Interview. Interview by author, 16 February 2011, Pasig City, MM, Philippines. Transcript in hand of author. Rodrigo Esperanza Documentary Project.
Ma, Wonsuk. "Philippines." In *The New International Dictionary of Pentecostal and Charismatic Movements*, rev. and exp. ed., ed. Stanley Burgess. Grand Rapids, MI: Zondervan, 2002.

Maggay, Melba P. *The Gospel in Filipino Context*. Mandaluyong City, Philippines: OMF Literature, 1987.

Malone, Robert. "The Assemblies of God and Its Program of Literature: Production and Distribution." *Pentecostal Voice*, October 1965, 7, 8.

[McCracken, Horace]. *History of Church of God Missions*. Cleveland, TN: Church of God Publishing House, 1943.

McGavran, Donald. *Multiplying Churches in the Philippines*. Manila: United Church of Christ in the Philippines, 1958.

McGee, Gary B. *This Gospel Shall be Preached*. Vol. 1: *A History and Theology of Assemblies of God Foreign Missions to 1959*. Springfield, MO: Gospel Publishing House, 1986.

Menzies, William W. *Anointed to Serve: The Story of the Assemblies of God, Vol. 1*. Springfield, MO: Gospel Publishing House, 1971.

Mercado, Leonardo N. *Elements of Filipino Philosophy*, rev. ed. In *Doing Filipino Theology*, ed. Leonardo N. Mercado. Asia Pacific Missiological Series, no. 6. Manila, Philippines: Divine Word Publications, 1997.

"Minutes of the General Council of the Assemblies of God, April 2-12, 1914." Flower Pentecostal Heritage Center CD Collection, Asia Pacific Research Center, Asia Pacific Theological Seminary, Baguio City, Philippines.

"Minutes of the General Council of the Assemblies of God, Oct. 1-7, 1916." Flower Pentecostal Heritage Center CD Collection, Asia Pacific Research Center, Asia Pacific Theological Seminary, Baguio City, Philippines.

"Minutes of the Seventh General Council of the Assemblies of God, Sept. 25-30, 1919." Flower Pentecostal Heritage Center CD Collection, Asia Pacific Research Center, Asia Pacific Theological Seminary, Baguio City, Philippines.

"Missionaries by Country." Flower Pentecostal Heritage Center, USAG Headquarters, Springfield, MO.

"A Missionary Movement." *Pentecostal Evangel*, 13 November 1920. Flower Pentecostal Heritage Center CD Collection, Asia Pacific Research Center, Asia Pacific Theological Seminary, Baguio City, Philippines.

Molina, Antonio M. *The Philippines through the Centuries*, vol. 2. Manila, Philippines: UST Cooperative, 1960.

Montgomery, James H., and Donald A. McGavran, *The Discipling of a Whole Nation*. Manila, Philippines: Philippine Crusades, 1980.

Montgomery, Jim. *New Testament Fire in the Philippines*. Manila, Philippines: Church Growth Research in the Philippines, 1972.

Newman, Joe. *Race and the Assemblies of God: The Journey from Azusa Street to the "Miracle of Memphis."* New York: Cambria Press, 2007.

"News Reports." *Bulletin*, June 1950, 6-7.

"News Reports." *Bulletin*, October 1952, 6.

"[No title], November 30, 1929." News clipping. Department of Foreign Missions Archives, USAG Headquarters, Springfield, MO.

Oconer, Luther. "The Manila Healing Revival and the First Pentecostal Defections in the Methodist Church in the Philippines." *Pneuma* 31 (2009): 66-84.

Oconer, Luther Jeremiah. "The *Culto Pentecostal* Story: Holiness Revivalism and the Making of Philippine Methodist Identity, 1899-1965." Ph.D. diss., Drew University, 2009.

Owens, Robert. "The Azusa Street Revival: The Pentecostal Movement Begins in America." In *The Century of the Holy Spirit: 100 Years of Pentecostal and Charismatic Renewal, 1901-2001*, ed. Vinson Synan. Nashville, TN: Thomas Nelson, 2001.

PDCAG. "Minutes of the Eighth Annual Convention, Philippines District Council of the Assemblies of God." Valenzuela City, Philippines: PGCAG Headquarters Archives, 1950.

_____. "Minutes of the First Annual Meeting of the Philippines District Council of the Assemblies of God, Inc." Valenzuela City, Philippines: PGCAG Headquarters Archives, 1940.

_____. "Minutes of the Seventh Annual Meeting of the Philippines District Council of the Assemblies of God." Valenzuela City, Philippines: PGCAG Headquarters Archives, 1949.

_____. "Minutes of the Sixth Annual Convention of the Philippine[s] District Council of the Assemblies of God." Valenzuela City, Philippines: PGCAG Headquarters Archives, 1948.

_____. "Philippines District Council of the Assemblies of God, Minutes of the Ninth Annual Convention." Valenzuela City, Philippines: PGCAG Headquarters Archives, 1951.

Perkin, Noel. Appointment Certification, 22 February 1946. Valenzuela City, Philippines: PGCAG Headquarters Archives, 1967.

PGCAG. "Business Session, Minutes of the Philippines General Council Convention." Valenzuela City, Philippines: PGCAG Headquarters Archives, 1959.

_____. "Minutes of the Fourth General Council Convention of the Assemblies of God." Valenzuela City, Philippines: PGCAG Headquarters Archives, 1961.

_____. "Minutes of the Philippines General Council of the Assemblies of God 1st Annual Convention." Valenzuela City, Philippines: PGCAG Headquarters Archives, 1953.

_____. "Minutes to the Sixth General Council Convention of the Philippines General Council of the Assemblies of God." Valenzuela City, Philippines: PGCAG Headquarters Archives, 1965.

_____. "Philippines General Council, Minutes of the Meeting." Valenzuela City, Philippines: PGCAG Headquarters Archives, 1963.

_____. "Philippines General Council of the Assemblies of God, Minutes to the Second General Council Convention." Valenzuela City, Philippines: PGCAG Headquarters Archives, 1956.

_____. "Proposed Amendments and Additions to the Constitution." Valenzuela City, Philippines: PGCAG Headquarters Archives, 1959.

_____. "Seventh General Convention, Philippines General Council of the Assemblies of God Minutes." Valenzuela City, Philippines: PGCAG Headquarters Archives, 1967.

R. C. Esperanza Obituary

Riss, Richard M. "Durham, William." In *The New International Dictionary of Pentecostal and Charismatic Movements*, rev. and exp. ed., ed. Stanley Burgess, 594-5. Grand Rapids, MI: Zondervan, 2002.

Robeck, Cecil M. Jr. *The Azusa Street Mission and Revival: The Birth of the Global Pentecostal Movement*. Nashville, TN: Thomas Nelson, 2006.

_____. "Azusa Street Revival." In *The New International Dictionary of Pentecostal and Charismatic Movements*, rev. and exp. ed., ed. Stanley Burgess, 344-50. Grand Rapids, MI: Zondervan, 2002.

_____. "Farrow, Lucy F." In *The New International Dictionary of Pentecostal and Charismatic Movements*, rev. and exp. ed., ed. Stanley Burgess, 632-3. Grand Rapids, MI: Zondervan, 2002.

_____. Foreword to *Asian and Pentecostal: The Charismatic Face of Christianity in Asia*, eds. Allan Anderson and Edmond Tang. Oxford: Regnum Books International, 2005.

_____. "Seymour, William Joseph." In *The New International Dictionary of Pentecostal and Charismatic Movements*, rev. and exp. ed., ed. Stanley Burgess, 1053-8. Grand Rapids, MI: Zondervan, 2002.

Rosario First Assembly of God Church. "Tribute to the Church Pioneer Pastor," 1969.

Sadorra, Eliseo M. "Asian Missionary Fact-Finding Report." *Pentecostal Voice*, June 1969, 10-11, 13.
Salazar, Dionisio S., and Lourdes C. Ungson. *Philippine Development and Progress*. Quezon City, Philippines: Taurus, 1974.
Sanneh, Lamin. *Translating the Message: The Missionary Impact on Culture*. American Society of Missiology Series, no. 13. Maryknoll, NY: Orbis, 1989.
Seleky, Trinidad E. "Six Filipinos and One American: Pioneers of the Assemblies of God in the Philippines." *Asian Journal of Pentecostal Studies* 4, no. 1 (2001): 119-129.
Seventh "7th General Council Convention, May 1-5, 1967." *Pentecostal Voice*, May 1967, 13-16.
Shemeth, Scott. "Ketcham, Maynard L." In *The New International Dictionary of Pentecostal and Charismatic Movements*, rev. and exp. ed., ed. Stanley Burgess, 821-2. Grand Rapids, MI: Zondervan, 2002.
Simpson, A. B. *The Gospel of Healing*, rev. ed. Harrisburg, PA: Christian Publications, 1915.
Sitoy, T. Valentino, Jr. *Several Springs, One Stream: The United Church of Christ in the Philippines*. Vol. 1, *Heritage and Origins (1898-1948)*. Quezon City: United Church of Christ in the Philippines, 1992.
_____. *SOS Manual*. Philippines: FARM, 2012.
"Southern Luzon District Holds First Mission Rally." *Pentecostal Voice*, October-November 1966, 6.
"Speed the Light." Available at http://stl.ag.org/about/, accessed December 6, 2012.
Stewart, Alexander C. "Bishop Clarence Lawson in the Pentecostal Assemblies of the World." Available at www.cooljc.org/LinkClick.aspx?fileticket=X0OkycfpTjc%3D&tabid=38&language=en-US, accessed February 7, 2013.
Suarez, Oscar S. *Protestantism and Authoritarian Politics*. Quezon City, Philippines: New Day, 1999.
Sumrall, Lester. *The True Story of Clarita Villanueva*. Manila, Philippines: by the author, 1955.
Synan, Vinson. *The Holiness-Pentecostal Movement in the United States*. Grand Rapids, MI: Eerdmans, 1971.
_____. *The Holiness-Pentecostal Tradition: Charismatic Movements in the Twentieth Century*, 2d ed. Grand Rapids, MI: Eerdmans, 1997.
_____. *In the Latter Days: The Outpouring of the Holy Spirit in the Twentieth Century*, rev. ed. Ann Arbor, MI: Vine Books, 1991.
_____. Introduction to *Azusa Street: The Roots of Modern-Day Pentecost*, by Frank Bartleman. South Plainfield, NJ: Bridge Publishing, 1980.
Tadina, Alicia Bautista. Interview by author, 24 March 2011, Pozorrubio, Pangasinan, Philippines. Transcript in the hand of author. Rodrigo Esperanza Documentary Project.
Tan, Michael L. *Usug, Kulam, Pasma: Traditional Concepts of Health and Illness in the Philippines*, eds. Lorna P. Makil and Mary Grenough. Traditional Medicine in the Philippines: Research Reports, no. 3. Quezon City, Philippines: Alay Kapwa Kilusang Pangkalusugan, 1987.
Texas Historical Commission. "Fundamentals of Oral History: Texas Preservation Guidelines." Available at http://www.thc.state.tx.us/publications/guidelines/OralHistory.pdf, accessed January 10, 2012.
"Trends Continue in Church Membership Growth or Decline, Reports 2011 Yearbook of American & Canadian Churches." Available at http://www.ncccusa.org/news/110210yearbook2011.html, accessed February 14, 2013.
The Trumpet 1964. Bethel Bible College school annual.

Trinidad, Ruben F. *A Monument to Religious Nationalism: History and Polity of the IEMELIF Church.* Quezon City: Evangelical Methodist Church in the Philippines, 1999.

Tuggy, Arthur. *The Philippine Church: Growth in a Changing Society.* Grand Rapids, MI: Eerdmans, 1971.

Wacker, Grant. *Heaven Below: Early Pentecostals and American Culture.* Cambridge: Harvard University Press, 2001.

Walls, Andrew F. *The Missionary Movement in Christian History: Studies in the Transmission of Faith.* Maryknoll, NY: Orbis, 1996.

"'The White Man's Burden': Kipling's Hymn to U.S. Imperialism." Available at http://historymatters.gmu.-edu/d/5478, accessed May 11, 2012.

Winehouse, Irwin. *The Assemblies of God: A Popular Survey.* New York: Vantage Press, 1959.

"Why Study Church History?" Available at http://www.christianitytoday.com/ch/1990/issue25/2541.html, accessed January 11, 2013.

"World Missions Department, Philippines General Council of the Assemblies of God." Available at http://pgcagwmd.wordpress.com/, accessed December 7, 2012.

Zeissler, Calvin. Interview by author, 5 April 2001, Transcript. APRC Oral History Collection, Asia Pacific Research Center, Asia Pacific Theological Seminary, Baguio City, Philippines.

Zeissler, Calvin R. "Profiles in Literature: Let Us Support Our Literature Program." *Pentecostal Voice*, May 1967, 10.

www.ingramcontent.com/pod-product-compliance
Lightning Source LLC
Chambersburg PA
CBHW071442150426
43191CB00008B/1201